INSIDE THE CHRISTIAN SCHOOL:
From the Headmaster's Diary

Roy W. Lowrie, Jr., Ed.D.

Headmaster
Delaware County Christian School
Newtown Square, Pa.

Foreword by Frank E. Gaebelein
Headmaster Emeritus
The Stony Brook School
Stony Brook, L.I.

Published by

Association of Christian Schools International
Box 4097, Whittier, California 90607

INSIDE THE CHRISTIAN SCHOOL:
From the Headmaster's Diary
© Copyrighted 1980, Roy W. Lowrie, Jr.
Printed in the United States of America

TO

Lucille Johnston
Maynard L. Gray
Frank H. Roberts
Alex Szucs

In honor of your 25 years of hearty service to God at the Delaware County Christian School, Newtown Square, Pa., 1955-1980.

"...I have learned by experience that the LORD hath blessed me for thy sake."

Genesis 30:27

45854

CONTENTS

Chapter 4

FOREWORD

It was a happy thought for Roy Lowrie to keep a diary of his days at the Delaware County Christian School and an even happier one to select these vignettes from his diary for publication in this book. In it we see what the life of a headmaster is really like. Here we have no mere job description but an honest portrayal of the joys and sorrows, frustrations and satisfactions of one of the most demanding tasks in education.

Dr. Lowrie writes about what makes education truly Christian —personal concern for students, teachers, and parents in the context of a school program rooted and grounded in Scripture and centered in Christ. He does this with biblically informed common sense expressed in unassuming words. While some proponents of evangelical education imply that a Christian school is a kind of utopia, Dr. Lowrie is too mature a headmaster to do this. He knows that the fact of a school's being Christian does not exempt it from its share of problems.

The integration of faith and learning is flawed unless it encompasses not only the curriculum but also the manifold relationships that make up the whole web of education. Piety and intellect are not incompatible. If a school is to grow in educating its students in knowledge and godliness, its head must know how to see policies and problems in the light of the Bible and bring them to God in prayer. One of the refreshing aspects of these pages is the naturalness with which Dr. Lowrie shares his devotional life with his readers.

Teachers, parents, and trustees will find this book of absorbing interest. As for young people of high school age, they will gain from it an understanding of a headmaster's concern for his students.

Frank E. Gaebelein
Headmaster Emeritus
The Stony Brook School

Preface

This has been a special year in my life. It was my 25th year as headmaster of D.C. Since it was a milestone, I decided to record some of it. This book is the result. Each day of the school year is not recorded for I could not keep up with it. With the exception of one page, each page is from the experiences of this symbolic year.

It is the purpose of the book to give an honest, candid viewpoint of the inside of a Christian school during a typical year. Since Christian schools face many things in common, it is hoped that some of the thoughts can be transferred to other schools in a helpful way.

Perhaps some of the experiences will help others realize that most of us are facing the same things. That is reassuring, for none of us is alone.

Although the style of writing is necessarily personal, it should be clearly understood on each page that God is totally involved in a Christian school day by day. Please understand that truth wherever it does not come through in the writing. The Scripture says that in Him we live and move and have our being. My confidence is in Him, only. (Psalm 62:5)

Roy W. Lowrie, Jr., Headmaster
Delaware County Christian School
Malin Road
Newtown Square, PA 19073

Chapter One

FACULTY ORIENTATION

Today was a moving experience for me. Our faculty and staff met for the first time in this new school year. There was excitement in the air as we greeted one another after the summer. It was good to see everyone.

Our first meeting was in room 213. We put the chairs in a large circle. After reading the Word and opening in prayer, we went around the circle sharing what we had done and what the Lord had been teaching us while we have been apart.

I had allowed unhurried time in our schedule for this first meeting. We had about two hours of very deep, quality fellowship. (I think that the best fellowship is talking about the Lord and praying to him.) The good hand of God upon us during the summer was obvious.

As people shared, I was quietly thanking God for leading each of us to D.C. to serve him. The working of the Spirit to bring us together as a unit has been clear. We come from different colleges and different parts of the country, but we are one. And, we are all born from above so we are fellow members of the body of Christ.

"Lord, thank you for a good start of good, hearty, fellowship today. Help us during the pressures of the year to keep the unity you have given us. Be honored among us each day, no matter what this year brings. Amen."

Dedication Service

Our annual dedication service was held in the gym tonight. I'm glad the founders of the school started this tradition of committing the year to God prior to the opening day of school. It is not a mechanical meeting, but a meaningful one. We are entering a new school year, one in which none of us has ever yet lived.

My soul was built up from the Word and from the exhortations of the speaker. The highlight for me, however, was the opportunity to introduce the faculty and staff to the parents. It was interesting to tell of their academic backgrounds and of their experience as teachers. (God has given us a quality faculty and staff.)

The new teachers and staff members each gave a two minute testimony of their salvation and of God's leading them to the school. This was heart-warming, encouraging.

I had joy in my heart, but a lump in my throat when Mrs. David King gave her testimony as a new teacher. I thank God for bringing her to serve him as a physical education teacher and coach. She knows the school well, for she is a graduate, having gone here from K-12. She also knows me well, for she is my daughter, Winnie. I'm looking forward to her ministry — and to the ministry of each new teacher.

A Good Bible Class

My Bible class went better than usual today. There were probably two reasons for that. First, I moved two girls from the back of the room to the front. I really should have done that long ago, but did not want to embarrass them. They certainly were intent today. They didn't seem to mind being up front.

Second, I did some role playing today and took the part of Abraham. It was stimulating to express his thoughts as he took Isaac up Mt. Moriah to offer him to the Lord. When I told how I felt upon finding the ram and substituting it for my son, the class was unusually sober. So was I, for the role had become very real for me. (I should role play more often and not lecture so much.)

Perhaps it was a good class because I myself was involved in the lesson with a high degree of feeling. That, I've noticed, makes a difference to my own enjoyment of teaching.

Part of my feeling was due to the emphasis of a great truth to my own spirit. This great truth was very fresh to me as I taught today: Since God performed all of his promises to Abraham, I can have complete confidence that he will perform all of his promises to me — and to my family. Oh, how I want my students and my own children, one of whom is in this Bible class, to believe that with all of their hearts.

Good and Bad Together

When a good thing happens, it seems to me that it is frequently followed by something bad. That occurred in my life again today. It is hard to go through the emotions of joy to the emotions of sorrow within a brief span of hours. I wonder why God allows life to be like that? Perhaps to prove that he can keep me on an even course no matter what a given day may bring.

I don't want to be on guard every time good things happen. But it would be unwise to drop all guarding, for then the sorrow could be debilitating. When the deep sadness comes, I want to still teach and administer effectively, from the position of God's strength, not mine. Many times only God and I know the exercise of my heart at that moment.

That is probably good, for it is not wise for me to tell everybody what is going on. My job requires confidentiality in many ways and in many instances. But this also means that I am having intimate experiences with God day-by-day that I do not often talk about.

"Thank you, Lord, for your good hand upon D.C., and upon me and my family."

The Body — Hurt and Happy

Today Peg and I went to the funeral of Lee's mother. Our faculty prayed for her since the day of her car accident, but she never regained consciousness. Several of our faculty and staff were there and I felt that Lee was glad we had come to share this intimate

3

experience with her. (The people in the other car were Christians. One knew Lee's mother. The pastor said it was God's way to take her home.)

The service was comforting. The sermon was on four prepositions. The Christian was born *without* Christ, upon salvation became *in* Christ, throughout life was *for* Christ, and upon death is *with* Christ. When the pastor concluded his comments on these prepositions he told us that this was the outline the pastor had used at the funeral of Billy Sunday. That caught my attention. (I like baseball and the Big Lake — Winona Lake, Indiana, the home of Billy Sunday.)

After the funeral Ivan and Emmagene invited Peg and me to join them to celebrate the 25th wedding anniversary of Elaine and Horace. We all had a lot of fun going to the Bird-in-Hand firehouse for a ham dinner. The fellowship was enjoyable and the meal was an experience.

Again, the Lord has shown me that our faculty and staff are a body. When one suffers, all of us suffer, and when one rejoices, all of us rejoice I cried with Lee in the afternoon, and laughed with Elaine and Horace in the evening. I Cor. 12 is so true, so applicable.

Peg is having some friends over to our home next week to surprise Elaine and Horace with a simple party.

A Teacher and Her Father

At faculty devotions this morning, Sue asked prayer for her father. She said that he was entering surgery in one hour to have a cyst removed from behind his right eye. Several of us prayed for him, and Peg prayed for Sue herself. Peg has learned what it is to suffer when loved ones are very sick, and usually prays for the persons who are well but are under those pressures which really can not be described.

I talked to Sue after the meeting and told her to feel free to leave school early to be with her father and the rest of the family. Those emergency times are important to families and I don't think her class would suffer if someone else covered for her. She said that she was leaving a little early, but that her father would be unconscious for most of the day and so she preferred to be in school. I'm certain that she experienced the grace of God and the strength of God in a deep way as she taught with all of these things on her heart. Her children are praying for her father.

(I just called Sue and the operation went well. It will be some time before the final results are known. Our faculty is pretty good at continuing in prayer for a matter like this. I feel satisfied that many will minister to Sue in this way. She will know that many people love her and care about her. It's not that she is insecure. It is just that through this pain she is going to get to know some of us on a deeper, more intimate level.)

God's Right Time

When I received the invitation today, my initial reaction was this: Lord, forgive me. Several years ago I was disappointed. I haven't brooded or felt bitter, but I have thought about the matter from time to time. It just didn't seem fair.

Now today something so special has been offered to me that it far supersedes the thing that I thought should happen two years ago. God's ways are above my ways and my times are in his hands.

This is not the first time that I have experienced this: God withholds something, but then later on gives something far better. (I need more patience to accept disappointments while waiting God's time.) That happens in school too. I remember being disappointed when we tried to buy property for the school and were turned down. That happened twice. But the property we finally got is far better than either of the ones we did not get.

There is one regret I have about the campus. I wish we had bought the whole 30 acres instead of 12. At the time we did not know what God was going to do. There was little money. Still, I'm sorry we did not have more vision. I think our people would have trusted God for the additional money.

Divine Guidance and Seniors

Had a good meeting this morning with six seniors — Bill, Pete, Tom, Dan, Ed, and Scott. We were talking about their plans for

5

enrolling in college. As we talked seriously I was aware that they were preoccupied with the championship game they were to play that afternoon. The timing of the meeting was not good for them.

They had many questions and much uncertainty. I encouraged them and told them that they would get the final answers on their knees. I think they believe me.

I can't tell how much this thought got through to them, but I encouraged them to trust God for future decisions too, saying that college decisions were only an example of what God will do for them all of their lives if they will trust Him. I care about these boys and their fellow seniors and all of their lives, not just from now until the day they graduate. If they graduate and then walk in disobedience to the Lord, the labor of their teachers will have been in vain. Paul cared a lot about the people he had served lest his work be in vain.

I also told them that I am seeking the Lord's will for decisions in my own life. Sometimes I think that students don't realize that teachers are doing the very things they are teaching about. I don't want to seem unreal to them.

A Prospective Student Teacher

Larry stopped to see me this morning. He is still a very open person. (I hope that never changes as he grows older.) We talked about his college work, especialy his plans for student teaching later in the year. Although he is in a secular college, it appears that he will be permitted to do some of his student teaching at our school. He did a practicum last year and our students loved him.

It hardly seems possible to me that he is a senior in college. It must be 6 or 7 years now that I've been encouraging him to train as a Christian elementary school teacher. We worked together several summers at a Christian camp. It was apparent that God had given him the gift of teaching. (I saw that years ago in Dave at camp, and this year he joined our faculty.)

Now that Larry is almost ready to join our ranks, I'm glad that he kept in touch with me over the years, for his college profs did not encourage him toward Christian school work. Our hours together during the past four years were well spent.

(God bless you, Larry. If we don't have room for you at D.C., some Christian School is going to get a great teacher. Maybe at a future date we will have just the opening for you.)

Saturday, and Long Range Planning

The meeting today was from 8 a.m. until 4 p.m., and I had to drive about 25 minutes each way. I wouldn't mind that so much, except it is Saturday. The Lord cleared my attitude before the meeting by reminding me that the school is my life, not my job. I'm not on a 40 hour week.

The day was profitable. The interchange of ideas flowed easily among the eight or so people in the group. It was wise to hold the meeting off-campus in new surroundings. There wasn't a single telephone call, not one distraction.

When the leader concluded the day, he said that we needed two more Saturdays like this before we would be ready to take our findings to the board. We looked at our calendars and set the dates well in advance.

I've never been in such an intense long range planning meeting and I've attended many over the years. It was good to have the long time, for we accomplished more than we could have in numerous two hour evening meetings.

The meeting sought God's guidance and was handled on a spiritual level. Yet as I drove home I was reminded of the Scripture that says, "...unless the Lord builds the house they labor in vain that build it." (I have to look up the reference for that. Is it marked in my Bible?)

An Important Principle

A new school father called me at home tonight. Last night, after a school event, I talked to him for a few minutes about some problems some students are having and said that his own son was among them.

In the course of our discussion I asked him to keep in touch with the teachers and with me instead of going straight to the board president as he had done with this matter. (The president called me and I didn't know anything about it.) I said that the chain of command was to the teacher, to the administration, to the education committee, and to the board. I also assured him that the problem was being dealt with.

He called me tonight because he said he was upset last night and today about our conversation. (I was not, thinking it was just an administrative principle that he did not understand.) He apologized and said that he had not meant to get me in trouble by going to the board president. I told him I was not in trouble, I only meant that in the future when problems come up that he should follow channels.

I'm glad he called. I wouldn't want him carrying a burden that does not even exist. I really expect that the two of us will have a very strong relationship because we have been able to talk over this matter.

Liberty in Faculty Devotions

At the conclusion of faculty devotions this morning I shared a concern with the group. Our faculty devotions are slowly becoming patterned. That is not good, for where the Spirit of the Lord is, there is liberty.

Some teachers do not participate enough. They tend to be the newer teachers which is understandable, yet this is not right for the faculty is a body and we all need each other. The body is nurtured by that which every joint supplieth. The comments and prayers of each person build up the whole group.

When I finished exhorting the faculty, I told them that this is one of the most difficult jobs of the headmaster. That is, they should all be involved but not because they feel pressured by me.

They listened well and accepted what I said. Time will tell whether it will be taken to heart. Spiritual change can not be mandated by the headmaster with teachers, or with students for that matter. It is a matter of the heart.

Although it is difficult, I must not draw back from encouraging the faculty in issues of this nature. It is my responsibility to speak the truth in love to encourage the unity and spiritual growth of the entire group. (I've long felt that Satan's greatest strategy and spear-head is always aimed at the faculty and staff.)

A Surprising Conference

This was an average administrative day, until my 2 p.m. appointment. I sensed that something was up when I got the phone call around 9 a.m. inviting me to lunch today. That was unusual for this person, out of character. Lunch was not possible on my schedule. (I may have made a mistake on that. Since the request was so unusual perhaps I should have juggled my other appointments and gone out to lunch. It is easier to talk at lunch for there is no telephone or people to talk to me. It is also more confidential, a neutral place.)

Before the 2 p.m. appointment I talked to several teachers at school to find out if there was a problem going with the students whose parents were coming to see me. I like to have as much background as possible going into a conference like that. Several things were told me, none of which seemed significant. I was relaxed.

The topic of the conference turned out to be a shock to me, a complete surprise. When it was over I stood by my back window for some time watching the elementary children getting their head, start for the afternoon buses, unnerved. I left school early because I couldn't think straight and did not feel like talking to anyone.

It won't take long before the whole school and Christian community know what was told me today about some of our students. Hard days lie ahead for them. Shame will come upon the school. I think though, that Jesus would not cut off a relationship with them because of their sin. That's why I'm not.

Encouragement to a Teacher

When school was about over today, I told my secretary that I would like to talk to a certain teacher when classes were dismissed. I had not mentioned this possibility to the teacher during the day and caught her off guard.

We sat down at the round table in my office and in a perplexed manner she asked me what I wanted. I said, "Do you need some money?" Her face fell, she was visibly moved. Her words were, "I feel like crying." She didn't, so I didn't have to get out the Kleenex box. We talked about it.

It turned out that she was under strong financial pressure. I had heard that she had a heavy car bill about two weeks ago. At the board meeting last Friday night (and morning, to 1:30 a.m., too long) one of the board members asked me if she had a need. Those two things prompted me to talk to her.

Tomorrow morning she will give me a request to borrow $350 from the faculty loan fund. I'll be sure to get that out to the head of the business committee, even though it is the last day before a vacation and is busy.

She thanked me for caring enough to talk to her about this personal matter. I believe that our relationship is good, but is now even stronger. Thank God that our board established this fund for emergency loans at no interest many years ago. God uses it to encourage the hearts of his servants over and over again.

A Faculty Morale Problem

There is an unusual morale problem going on with part of the faculty. It is hard to solve because it has to do with teaching load. It is not the fault of the teacher around whom it centers, for he did not make out the teaching assignments. A principal did that.

Although it is an administrative mistake, ultimately mine as head of the school even though I didn't know about it at the time, it was not done the way it turned out. The teacher had another course on his original schedule, but it was canceled the first week of school because the enrollment was too low to warrant it for the year. He will pick up another course at the start of the second semester, and perhaps a short-term course before then.

The teachers are aware of what each does even though they don't talk to me or the principals very much about it. I just hope that the explanation of how this happened will stop any further talk. There are enough problems without adding this, which was not deliberate.

That parable about the vineyard workers who all got the same pay when some worked all day and others a half day sometimes bothers me, for it was not fair. Yet the other side of that is what Jesus emphasized which was: If you agree to work for a set amount it is none of your business what others do for their pay. (Boy, that is a strong thought. I'd like to teach that without people thinking I was cramming it down their throats to cover a problem.)

A Sick Parent

Bill is in surgery at this moment. His family has been in the school for years. I called him yesterday afternoon to express my concern and to assure him that many were praying. Last night the school prayer chain was activated for him. Preliminary tests indicate that he has a growth in his esophagus that extends into his stomach. It is malignant. (Lord, guide the hands of the surgeon. Great Physician, heal Bill.)

This matter seems unusual to me. The reason is this: Bill himself is a renowned physician. It is hard to think of such a remarkable doctor needing a doctor himself.

Something keeps striking me through this. It is not easy to sort my thoughts out, but this is what is on my heart: I hope that our faculty, students, and parents don't perceive me as not needing spiritual help daily. I need daily cleansing for sin even as doctors need doctors themselves, even though I am in a spiritual work. I don't serve the school from a position of spiritual superiority, although I am the administrative and educational leader.

I remember the first year I came to D.C. Every day at prayer time, Don, one of the sixth grade boys prayed out loud for me. He always said, "Dear Lord, please give Mr. Lowrie the wisdom and knowledge to teach us today." I still need exactly that.

Counseling My Son

My son gets home from college for vacation tomorrow night. Peg, his sisters and I are so eager to see him. It's been a long time. He is so far away that we seldom are together.

We all need time together, but I see that we also need to talk with him alone. Peg needs to talk with him to satisfy her mother's heart and to counsel him from a mother's perspective. Beth needs his counsel as her older brother. Ellen needs to talk to him as his older sister. We are all in this together. (Winnie and Janet will not be home.)

I need to talk to him alone too. I don't plan to spend much time asking him what he is doing. I want to spend our personal time together asking him what he is thinking. (He doesn't write enough. My folks told me that, too, when I was overseas and at college years ago.)

We have to talk about God's working in his life. About the Scriptures that are upon his heart. About next summer. About long range plans. About values. About life. About girls. About decisions facing me.

Peg and I have no worldly ambitions for him or for his sisters. We want each to do God's will, and to come to know the Lord well. Period.

I care deeply that I not miss out in the raising of my own children by being so busy in the school that I neglect my own children. I am their father and God has put on me in particular and on Peg the sacred responsibility to raise them in the nurture and admonition of the Lord.

"Lord, give us a great vacation together."

Inexorable Downward Pressures

I've been thinking today about a discussion in which I was involved last night. The discussion gave me some deep insight as to how some of the people feel about an issue which is very significant in the life of the school. I knew how some felt, but some others surprised me quite a bit. It was apparent that some of my assumptions were wrong when I had quite a bit of confidence that they were right.

The matter has shown me again that there is enexorable pressure upon me to lower standards, to relax, to ease off, to let down. Actually that would be the easiest thing to do. Perhaps I would be more popular. But, I can't go against that which I believe is of the Lord, in the life of the school or in my own life. I purpose to please him, hoping that people will understand. If they don't, I still want to please him. The day is coming when I'll answer directly to him.

This issue has reminded me of Dr. Frank Gaebelein's advice to me quite a few years ago. I was visiting Stony Brook and seeking his counsel. The thing I have remembered over the years was this, "Roy, there are two things you must control to have a Christian school. They are the student body and the faculty."

How many times that counsel has helped me! How much prayer, courage, will power, and diligence are needed to control both!

Renewal of Accreditation

Our high school is up for the renewal of our accreditation with the Middle States Association of Colleges and Secondary Schools. Last night we had a dinner for the 12 man visitation committee, our board officers, and our department heads. Our board president welcomed the committee. I spoke to them about our history, philosophy, and objectives, and the high school principal described the school and the community. The evening went well, a good start.

The faculty has worked hard for a year in self evaluation in preparation for this three day visit. We are ready, but there is some tension about having so many visitors for three days in a row. It should develop poise in all of us as we work under these pressures.

One of the teachers told me this afternoon that he thinks the self evaluation is more meaningful than the visiting committee. There is truth to that, for we have been forced to take a long, hard, objective look at the school. It is also true that outside educators can be used of God to bring out other aspects of the school which are good or which need to be improved. (I'm committed to improvement.)

I've been thinking, this is the third time I've gone through the accreditation with our high school and I've gone through the accreditation of our elementary school another three times. Accreditation is important to me, but it is not the same as God's approval. Actually the Spirit is on campus every day. We all need to be sensitive to him in our teaching, in our counseling, in all aspects of school life.

An Injured Student

The school nurse called my office late in the morning to say that one of our junior high boys had a deep cut on his forehead from phys ed class and needed stitches. She was calling his parents to see which hospital they wanted him taken to. She was also arranging transportation help to get him there.

I stopped what I was doing and went straight to the nurse's office. The bleeding had stopped. He showed me the cut. It was almost in the middle of his forehead, and it was deep. It was a clean cut, not ragged, and it should heal without much of a scar. I quietly asked God to guide the hands of the doctor who would be sewing him up. I prayed that no welt of scar tissue would form.

Although I did not go to the hsopital with him (I would have if it had been more serious), he knows that I am sorry that this happened. He knows that I care for him. I know him by name. We belong to each other.

As soon as they left for the hospital, I went over to the gym and talked to the teacher to find out how it happened. It occurred in a controlled situation and from all appearances it was an unforseeable accident. Even so, I talked briefly but strongly to the teacher about safety. We've been having a rash of semi-serious accidents lately and I can't tell whether we need to tighten up, or whether we are in an unavoidable string of accidents that sometimes cluster together. Anyway, the teacher assured me that he would do his best to be careful. We need to pray more about safety, not just for traveling mercies.

God Working in a Senior

The last hour of the school day was easily the best for me. My secretary told me that one of the senior girls wanted to talk to me, for she had a study hall then. I had no inkling of what she would say. I enjoy that, though, because administrative work sometimes bores me because it is so patterned, so predictable.

To my delight, she said that she thinks God is leading her to be a missionary. She asked my counsel about schooling, about short term missionary service, about some things in the Christian life. We both had a lot of freedom in the Lord and talked openly and heart-to-heart about numerous things. It was an exceptional hour. I'm so glad that she wanted to see me.

It would not be right to try to measure the school by the number of graduates who are missionaries. We have a goodly number now who serve God in America and around the world. The real question is this: How many of the graduates are doing God's will for them?

At the same time, Jesus said to lift up our eyes to the harvest. It is ready, but the laborers are few. He said to pray that God would send forth those laborers. It is clear to me that many should come from our school.

Over the years I've observed that many who talk about the mission field never get there. But, some do.

"Lord, may this girl be in that number who take the gospel to those who sit in darkness in other countries."

Budget Cuts

I've received a note from the school treasurer. He is asking me to make recommendations for cutting $13,000 out of the current operating budget. I understand his request, for our enrollment came in 13 short of our projections on which this budget was based. Also, gift money is not coming in as well as we had projected.

I don't like to have to cut the educational accounts in the budget. Yet I agree with his note and see the need to do this. We must guard against going into debt on the operating budget. Once I saw a fine school almost go under because they started to borrow money for the operating budget and found it hard money to repay. I started to see what could be cut today, but want to wrestle with this one for at least a week, rather than give a quick answer. I don't think the entire $13,000 should come from my accounts.

This matter brings up the issue of not cutting budget, but just trusting God to bring it all in. In my heart I like that idea, but it must be balanced with the Scriptural injunction to count the cost before you begin, to be sure that you can finish.

It is different to live by faith for myself and for my family. Peg and I have seen God do remarkable things for us and for our children when we had no money but felt that God wanted us to move ahead on something. Yet the school operates on a kind of corporate faith, while our family operates on our own faith. It appears that it is hard for some businessmen to decide things by faith.

God's Presence on Campus

Our reading for faculty devotions this morning was Hebrews 13. I've always loved that book since I studied under a Bible teacher who loved that book and transmitted it to me.

The benediction at the close of the chapter is my favorite benediction among all of the great ones in the Scripture. It ends with teaching that to Christ is to be glory forever and ever. My heart responded especially to that today for this reason.

Yesterday a visitor who had been with us for several days spoke to the faculty at the close of the school about some of his impressions. He was not a Christian. He was visibly moved as he described us as a unique school among the many that he had observed. He spoke of the dedication of the faculty, the hard work of the faculty, the good personal relationships within the school, the fine student body, the good facilities, the fine upkeep, etc.

Then he said, "The presence of God on this campus is palpable. You can feel him." My heart leaped, and I quietly praised the Lord. It was a rich experience for me and for my colleagues. Everyone was still, sober.

When it was my turn to comment on Hebrews 13 this morning, I reminded the faculty of what this man had said yesterday. Then I acknowledged that the credit, the glory, belong to Jesus Christ, not to us. God has worked in us both to will and to do of his good pleasure. We work hard, but God gives the increase. The praise is his, alone.

My spirit is greatly encouraged to realize that this man recognized that the unique thing about the school is God.

Contact from a Graduate

The phone rang here at home about 2:30 this afternoon. I was glad that I hadn't yet started my usual Sunday afternoon nap. (Thank God for Sunday afternoon naps.) It was good that I was wide awake to understand the caller.

The caller is one of our graduates from several years back. In a remarkable way, the relationship between the two of us has not only continued over the years, but it has become stronger. I have no authority over him as in his school days, so we share together as brothers in Christ. (He probably doesn't know that I too enjoy that change in our relationship, for there are times when I get tired of being in the place of authority.)

For several months the two of us have been sharing about a particular problem. It is now intense and I'm not at all sure what is going to be the outcome. We talked it over for a while.

When he told me that I am his friend and that he is counting on me to pray, I assured him that I would and that he was welcome to call me or to come see me at any time. He knows that I mean those words.

Epaphras of the Bible has long been an example to me of a person who had a continuing interest in people, even after he was no longer with them. He prayed that they would stand perfect and complete in all of the will of God.

"Lord, I ask that for this graduate at this hard time."

Letter to the Mailing Lists

This morning I wrote a letter to the people on our different mailing lists. Those are not easy letters for me to write, for they are really requests for money.

I've gone to different seminars to learn how to write appeal letters. The statistics at those seminars are impressive as to which letters draw more responses. Yet I have some conflict in my mind and in my conscience about some of this. For example, is it right to deliberately trigger a gift from a donor by clever writing when the Lord loves a cheerful giver? Or is that really helping the donor to lay up treasure in heaven? The answers I've heard don't satisfy my mind and heart deep down.

The letter I wrote was just a straightforward note from my heart to others about the school. I asked them to give and I asked them to pray. If there is a response, it will be from God and my conscience is clear because I did not wheedle anything out of anyone by my writing.

I remember visiting the office of the treasurer of O.M.F. Painted on the wall opposite the treasurer's desk is that thought of Hudson Taylor, the founder of the mission. This may not be the exact quote but it is at least very close: "God's work done in God's way will have God's provision." That rings the bell with me. I believe that. I believe Matthew 6:33 for my family and also for the school.

Recognition of Weaknesses

The Middle States visiting committee completed three days of evaluation this afternoon. At 3:30 the chairman gave an oral report to the faculty and administration. It was quite positive. (I've learned to be somewhat reserved, however, until we get the written report. That is the one that counts — and I've had the experience of a chairman slipping some strong comments into the written report that he did not say in the oral report.)

He complimented our faculty for our honesty in our self evaluations. He said that he had been chairing committees for 18 years, and his committee made fewer changes on the ratings made by our faculty than on any school he had ever visited. In saying this he gave us the comment of a committee member who said, "You have to hand it to them. These people are honest."

I'm pleased by this. At the same time, it makes something very apparent to me. It is this: We can be quite accurate in analyzing the strengths and the weaknesses of the school without outside help. The outside help has been a service to us by emphasizing what we already know and by encouraging us to get busy and resolve the weaknesses of the school. But we know our school's problems well.

(I remember that I was stung 10 years ago by the comment of another committee when we were up for renewal of accreditation. That committee said that we should get to work and solve our problems and not just pray about them and then tolerate them.)

Too Busy a Day

This has been an unusually hectic day. I knew it would be busy, but not this busy. It began on a somber note as I took a few minutes at the end of faculty devotions to talk to the faculty about three serious issues that have converged upon us at once, none of which is of our own doing, but each of which affects every last one of us.

First period Bible class went well. I taught them some things from the Word that few of them knew before, and that was rewarding. There's something about teaching Bible that beats teaching any other subject.

After that I felt that I was trapped in a revolving door. A visitor came to talk to me about the school, a reporter came for an interview, an administrator talked to me about a serious mistake in the schedule which had to be resolved at once, the phone kept ringing, I had to make a tape recording, the mail was heavier than usual, I was late to an appointment, etc.

All day I've been thinking about the comment one of our teachers shared when it was his turn to share from the Word this morning. He said, "God always gives us the time to do the things that he wants us to do." That strikes a response down in me. It just doesn't seem right for a headmaster or a teacher to be as under the gun as I have been today. At the same time, I'm not sure what to do about it, because all of it was not of my doing except that I talked to someone longer than I expected about a spiritual matter. Was that wrong? Isn't that what the school is all about?

An Opportunity to Share Christ

Some years ago I promised the Lord that when he brought an unsaved person to my office and opened the conversation to spiritual things, I would not hide the gospel from that person but would talk to him about his soul. Today I kept that promise again. (I have missed some over the years to my regret. There is no way to recapture those misses.)

A young mother came to visit the elementary school this morning. She visited almost every class and then stopped to talk with me. She is probably a good mother. It was obvious that she loves her children and that she wants the best schooling for them.

As we talked it was clear that she was religious, but that she did not know the Lord. She was willing to talk about the new birth. As we did, it was also clear that God is at work in her heart. His power and presence were stronger than usual.

She did not receive Christ, but she is on the verge. I know it is not in me to reveal to her that Jesus is the Christ. That realization does not come from flesh and blood, but from the Father. We are going to talk more about Christ next week. That's something good to look forward to. (Often I'm looking forward to problems.)

It's remarkable to realize that through the school God ministers to parents as well as to children and teenagers.

"Father, open her heart to receive Christ. Then, do the same for her husband and children."

Stealing from Within

There is a rash of stealing going on in the school. For some reason this bothers me more than a lot of other things which are wrong. Part of it is probably because parents and some officials think that stealing could be found out easily. They don't realize how hard it is to find out who is doing it. (Maybe I should have gone to summer school at Scotland Yard to become a better sleuth.)

We have been praying that God would bring these people, or this individual to light. He knows, but we do not. People are starting to get up tight.

Yesterday one of our faculty members had $40 stolen out of his wallet, which was in his car out on the parking lot. That is so different from the other stealing which has focused on the locker room (the girls, to my surprise) that the matter is all the more perplexing.

I suggested to the faculty that we take a love offering in two days for the teacher who lost the $40, for that loss would hurt him and his family. This way we will all suffer a small loss instead of one of us suffering a big loss. The suggestion was well received. Heads were nodding and teachers were smiling.

(Won't it be something if the love offering amounts to more than $40? That would be great, a genuine token of our love for him and his family. We will take the offering in an envelope and I will give it to him without counting it. I'm looking forward to giving to this.)

Circumstances Indicate Guilt

About noon a teacher apprehended a student with an object that had been stolen a few days ago. The student claimed no knowledge of the matter, but had the object in possession. There is no way to know whether or not the student has been involved in the other stealing incidents.

It is hard to discipline a student who claims innocence, but circumstances indicate guilt. There is no repentance, no remorse. What is there to build on? Maybe the student is not a Christian. (Although Christianity is claimed.)

The father will be called tonight and will come in to school tomorrow or the next day. Perhaps he can help us to understand. Perhaps we can also help him to understand. I hope so. Professional counseling beyond the abilities of our faculty seems to be in order, but I doubt that the family can afford it. What can we do? The teachers are at the frustration threshold. Even the teacher who has the best relationship with the student has run out of ideas.

Our discipline procedures don't seem to really fit in this situation. Yet if discipline is tempered, would that be fair to other students who have been disciplined strongly for lesser things? Would that be partiality or would that be the right thing to do in this case? I'm inclined toward tempering.

"Lord, give wisdom to everyone involved."

Concerns about Music Performances

The elementary choir had a concert this week. The high school choir schedule for outside engagements is almost full. Both choirs are good and people like them. They are impressive. Today I talked with one of the directors.

In my heart I have a concern about the performances. It has to do with the fine line between using the choir as public relations, hoping that people will like them and give more money to the school, or using the choirs to promote worship alone.

21

I believe that the school needs to stay well on the side of promoting worship alone. If the musicians honor God, he will send us the students and the money which we need to subsist and to grow. To do less would be using the students.

It's not easy to teach these concepts to students when they are so enthusiastic about the school. That is part of the job of the choir leaders, and they'll have to keep working on it.

Some churches are going to have some good choir members in a few years. I hope our graduates move into those choirs with good hearts, understanding their music as a ministry. I also hope that they move in with well trained voices. (Some church choirs need a boost.)

Advance Preparation by God

I received a real "hate" letter in the mail today. Unlike some in the past, this one was signed. It amazed me that the writer, whom I know, would write such a strong letter. It is so mean I don't plan to show it to Peg, for it would upset her.

The letter includes falsehoods, innuendos, and harsh language. Although I try to keep up with correspondence, I've decided not to answer this. It would only lead to further correspondence and more letters of the same spirit. There's no value in that.

Just yesterday in the Word I was reading about entrusting myself to God who judges righteously. Little did I realize that an unrighteous judgment was already in the mail with my name on it.

It's interesting to note how many times the Lord impresses something on my heart from the Scripture in advance of the situation where I must claim that Scripture. That is an evidence that God watches out for me as my Dad watched out for me when I was growing up. It is also an evidence of the inspiration of Scripture. Here is a book written centuries ago which is so relevant that it is comparable to a newly published book with the latest copyright.

(I've had enough for one day, but have a committee meeting tonight. I need a few hours of respite.)

Below Par and Caution

I'm quite tired today. The meeting last night was rather long. More than that, it was difficult. It took a lot out of me emotionally. It was even hard to fall asleep, which is unusual.

Since I know I'm not up to par today, I don't plan to make any big decisions. I've learned to be cautious and somewhat reserved on hard days like this. I don't want to make some mistake just because I'm not feeling well enough to think straight. Mistakes are not reversed because they were made under duress.

There is no fretting on my part and I'm not holding any bitterness in my heart. It's just that I don't feel so hot because I didn't get enough sleep.

My soul was refreshed from being with everyone in faculty devotions this morning. This turned out to be one of the three or four mornings per year when we all come a half an hour early to have coffee and cake before we read the Word and pray. It was good fellowship and there was liberty among us as we commented together on today's chapter. The closing hymn sounded like a choir.

The Lord is gracious. Knowing that I needed a boost today, he gave me the strengthening that comes from the fellowship of the saints.

Ministry of My Secretary

My secretary was obviously sick with a heavy cold this morning, so I sent her home as soon as she would go. She should not have come in at all, but is extremely conscientious. I can always depend on her.

Her absence caused me to reflect on her ministry to the school, and to me. In addition to being a top-flight executive secretary, she is a Christian lady with all of the graces that that implies. She is faithful, loyal, discerning, discreet, and strong. Her commitment to Christian education is deep. She understands what the school is all about. That understanding undergirds much of the work which she does.

It's strange, but some people think that a Christian school secretary does not work as hard as a secretary in industry. Over the years I have had several secretaries in the various offices of the school who had considerable experience in industry. Everyone said that the work of the school was more demanding. They should know, for they have held jobs in both.

Our staff members are the unsung heroes. Without them the school could not function. That is why they are all included along with all of the teachers from K-12 in the processional and recessional at senior commencement. That is our way of honoring them publicly. We are saying to the graduates that all of these people had a part in bringing them to the point of graduation.

Chapter Two

MATTHEW 18
IN THE SCHOOL

This morning I saw a copy of a letter which a parent sent directly to the board. It is a letter of complaint about two of the teachers. Neither parent talked to the teachers, to the elementary school principal, or to me. All of us were bypassed.

This is an important administrative issue to me. We tell our parents to follow the teaching of Matthew 18. If you have a problem, talk to the teacher involved. If you aren't satisfied talk to the principal of the elementary school or of the high school. If you aren't satisfied, talk to the headmaster. If you aren't satisfied, take it to the education committee. If you aren't satisfied, take it to the board.

Now that all of this has been breached, it will be interesting to see how the board will handle it. I hope that they stick to what they tell all incoming parents about following the procedures outlined. Yet I know that some board members want parents to come directly to them. They don't realize the damage which that does to the position of the teacher. You can't teach if you have to worry about parents bypassing you and the administration by taking a matter straight to the board.

If this comes up, and it probably will at the board, I'm going to speak up about the procedure even though I know some board members won't agree. (I don't look forward to that.)

Tight Finances

Tonight at the regular meeting of the business committee of the board we found that the financial status of the school is not strong. There is money for the next payroll, but not much more. If I didn't know the Lord, I'd be upset.

I was instructed about a month ago to restrict purchases. Many purchases were already in the pipeline, though, and the invoices are coming due. It takes time before restrictive moves are reflected in the financial reports.

The tuition payments are coming in reasonably well without too much deficit. The problem lies in the area of gifts to the school from our present families and from donors outside of the school. The current budget was constructed carefully, but gift income is far below the budgeted amount. The committee discussed several approaches to the problem and plans to make recommendations to the board later this week.

I don't really know what to do. I do know where to look. This school belongs to God and he is the ultimate Source of all of our funds, both tuition money and gift money. My expectation is from him.

I'm reminded of the time a man asked me who I called when the school had a serious financial need. I chuckle as I recall the look on his face when I asked him if he knew God's telephone number —Jer. 33:3. I've never called a wealthy man to meet our needs and I don't intend to start now.

"Lord, give the school this day our daily bread."

The Spiritual Is Practical

Jeremiah 33:3 works. This afternoon the bookkeeper came into my office to show me a check which has just come in for regular operating expenses. It was for $5,300, a large amount for the school. Most of our gift checks are for less than $100.

A few days ago one of our school fathers made the comment that the spiritual is always practical. I believe that. Living by biblical principles is always practical. It has to be the devil who makes us think otherwise, for he is the father of lies. Questioning the principles of Scripture certainly does not come from God.

I've been thinking about the Old Testament people who raised the question, "Can God set a table in the wilderness?" Many times during the year that text has come to me. The answer is "yes," and that without any reservation. He is able — today.

Praise the Lord, I've always been paid in full and on time with one exception. In that one exception there was a mistake in bookkeeping. The Lord had provided the money, but we all were paid a day late because the books were gummed up and it appeared that the checks would bounce if issued.

Yet it takes faith each day for the school to operate. That's spiritually healthy, for it keeps us from thinking that we can finance it on our own without Divine provision. (I wonder if the new teachers understand this?)

Unscheduled Payday

One of our graduates sent me a 3 x 5 card today with the following written on it:

Dear Dr. Lowrie,

I'm really thankful for the great time I had at D.C. My high school memories will never be forgotten. I'm supporting D.C. with my whole heart! Thank you for all the prayers and preparation you and the other teachers had undertaken. I really appreciated it!

In Christ,
Kim

Now, this is payday. Oh, it isn't the 15th or the 30th when I get my school check. But this is the kind of pay that means more than money. How encouraging it is to my spirit to get a short note like that.

Perhaps my joy is also related to the fact that notes like that seldom come to me from graduates or from parents. If I were a headmaster because I wanted the praise of men, I would have stopped long ago, for few express appreciation. That is not a complaint. It is simply the way that it is. (I'm impressed that when Jesus healed ten lepers at once, only one came back to thank him, and that

one was a Samaritan.) I serve God with my eye on a future day —
when I will be with Christ.

An Awkward Bypass

My board president called me this afternoon to tell me something
he had heard that had happened at school. It caught me by surprise,
for I had not heard a word about it, and it was a reasonably
significant matter. (I deeply dislike being in that position, for it
makes me look as if I don't know what's going on at the school. At
the same time, I don't always know what has happened, and it is
better to know with embarrassment than not to know.)

When he hung up, I checked the schedule of the teacher whom he
mentioned and caught him between periods. Lo and behold, it was
exactly as the president reported it to me. I asked the teacher in the
future to please come and tell me when things of this magnitude
occur instead of talking about it to others.

I'm not sure I handled it too well because I was irritated. It
probably would have been better to wait until after school when we
would have had some more time.

The teacher is one of the most professional on the faculty. He
apologized, and assured me that it would not happen again. I believe
him. I also believe that our relationship is strong enough to weather
the present stress. (He was in our home recently, and we had a great
evening.)

A Sandwich and Spirituality

I had a good laugh followed by a sober thought over an incident
brought to my attention today. It's hard to believe, but the whole
thing was over a salami sandwich traded at lunch in an elementary
class. Jimmy brought the salami sandwich in his lunch and traded it
to Mike, not at all unusual. However, Mikey sniffed at the sandwich
and called off the trade with the words, "This sandwich stinks."

Well, Jimmy went home and told his mother what Mike said
about the sandwich, and she got upset. This morning she called the
teacher about it and said that Mike's attitude was totally unchristian
and that she should do something about it, get him into shape.

Sometimes I really wonder what some parents expect of children. Is it actually sin for a child to say that a salami sandwich stinks? If it is, I'm really in trouble because I think that salami stinks a little myself, even though I eat a salami sandwich once in a while. (I never order it, however.)

Isn't it overriding the nature of a child like Mikey to reprove him for a thing like this, making it out to be a Christian issue? Is it fair to Jimmy to let him think that the honest response of Mikey was unchristian?

(Cheers for parents! Lord help us teachers!)

Crushing News

It is not unusual for me to get a letter in the mail which is marked "personal." Today's mail included such a letter in a light blue envelope. I didn't think too much of it as I opened it for I recognized the name in the upper left-hand corner.

The letter was short, only two sentences. The first sentence said what had happened and the second sentence asked me to pray. The contents of the letter stunned me. One of our graduates has been sentenced to jail, and his mother wants me to pray. I know them well.

My heart is grieved, deeply. What has happened? When was it? Where? What prison is he in? How can I reach him? Could I visit? Would he even want to see me under the circumstances? Whatever it was, why did he do it?

My numerous phone calls to the mother today went unanswered. She must be away. What can I do for her?

Should I tell the faculty? The board? (I think for now I'll keep it between Peg and me. The two of us will pray and act. The word will get around quickly enough.)

"Lord, show me the way in this matter. Part of me is locked up with him. Please, let there be rehabilitation. Even more, please let there be restoration. Help us strongly, dear Father in heaven."

A Family Withdraws

A father came to see me this morning to inform me that he is withdrawing his children from the school for financial reasons.

Knowing that finances are sometimes a coverup for other reasons, I questioned him and feel that it is a genuine financial problem.

Although I don't know him well, the Lord gave the two of us an unusual openness as we talked seriously about spiritual matters. I learned that his family is facing a serious spiritual issue that has nothing to do with the school.

When we were concluding our time together, I assured him of my continued interest and prayers on behalf of him and his family. I told him that our Christian fellowship did not depend on the enrollment of his children in the school, but is based upon the fact that we both belong to Christ. That comment appeared to surprise him somewhat. I invited him to keep in touch, and he said he was heartened, encouraged, by that invitation. I hope that he will.

Families which drop out of the school often say that they will be back. I've observed, though, that returnees are infrequent. I hope this family returns. They need the school. They also need a good home church. (I have a growing concern: It seems that more and more families are not going to solid Bible-believing churches. I can't understand that. It hurts the parents and the children.)

Professional Appearance

Before school this morning I spoke privately to one of our male teachers about his appearance. I told him that I wanted him to dress more appropriately for school. I reminded him that he was a professional educator and should present himself in a good manner.

To my surprise, my counsel to him struck fire. He reacted very negatively to what I had said, implying that it wasn't too important how he looked. (He thinks he looks pretty good, and he does compared to the way he dressed in college. That is not a good standard for comparison.) I did not back down and was firm in telling him to improve, even though he said that he can not afford to.

Part of this was my fault, for I should have spoken to him several weeks ago. By letting the matter slide for a while, it made it appear that I approved of his appearance. My words caught him off-guard and it seems that his overreaction was a defense mechanism. (I always get hurt somehow when I let a matter slide with the hope that it will self-correct. Most administrative matters are not self-correcting.)

Although our relationship is hurt today, I believe that it is deep enough and strong enough to stand this strain. I'm sorry to have hurt him.

Be Not Many Coaches

I guess that the telephone is a good invention, but sometimes I wish I had an office without one. For example, today I got a rather irate call from a school father which has presented me with an administrative problem. It has to do with varsity sports.

The father complained that his child is not getting enough playing time. He had talked to the coach about it previously. The call was triggered by the fact that yesterday his child was the only one not to play, a very personal matter. "Roy, are we building character or do we only try to win games?"

After he had talked for quite a while I recommended that he invite the coach out for dinner to give the two of them a chance to talk heart-to-heart. Communication of ideas and feelings is needed so there can be healing in this matter.

We do play to win in the interscholastic program. While doing this, I have asked the coaches to play as many students as possible. It seems that most coaches were good athletes themselves and were usually starters. They don't know what it is like to ride the bench game after game. This father has a point and deserves to be heard. (At the same time, I can't picture my own Dad talking to any of my coaches or administrators about my interscholastic career. I was on my own. That's the way I have been with my own children too. Coaches should play to win.)

A Team Complimented

Things continue to come in twos. Today I received a very good report about one of our interscholastic teams. It was reported in the faculty meeting as an item for praise that a referee who had worked a game involving our girls' basketball team said that she had never seen a team with such personal standards and good sportsmanship.

It is possible, then, to build character and still play hard to win.

Sometimes I think we don't recognize what God is doing in the lives of our students for we work only with them and so compare them with themselves rather than with their peers who attend secular schools. To illustrate, yesterday's paper had an article about an athletic team from a nearby school which vandalized their bus while returning from an away game to the sum of $2,000, and our high school administrator is in a sweat about writing on bathroom partitions.

I don't condone that writing, but in perspective it is a minor thing. The gospel does work in the life of a student. Here an outside referee working our game at another school saw the difference in our girls. That's great. The girls need to be told about this. It is a credit to them and to their coach.

(I wonder what the refs think about our boys' teams. I hope they detect a difference there too.)

Freedom in Conference

My 2 p.m. appointment today had been on my calendar for about a week. I was not looking forward to it because it was about a problem which I had been watching closely for at least six weeks. The appointment was with the parents of one of our students. I have known them for several years.

They had gone to the teacher about a matter. They were not satisfied with their discussion, and wrote a letter about their child and the teacher. The chairman of the education committee was given a copy of the letter, but steered the parents to talk to the teacher and the elementary principal next. (Thank the Lord for such supervision in our administrative chain of command.)

Well, the parents still weren't satisfied, so today they met with me, the next procedural step. Our chain of command is effective, and I seldom have this kind of a conference. That's why I was apprehensive.

It was a case of being anxious for nothing. We all had great freedom in the conference and appeared to have a good meeting of the minds. (Time will certainly be needed to tell about that.) God gave me some new ideas in the matter.

We closed with a word of prayer, looking to God for his working. Of course, they want the best and so do we at school — all for the child. The Matthew 18 principle is a wondrous thing to experience.

Bible Class Ends Incomplete

This morning I taught my Bible class for the last time. (I don't have them for the entire year.) It was nostalgic for me, for I've enjoyed my hours with them in the Word. It has been good for me — and I hope for them.

We accomplished a lot this semester, but I'm conscious that there is so much more to do. Yet I think that is always the way it is when it comes to teaching Bible. By the very nature of the Book you never feel that you are done. I look forward to having them again next year.

A special thing regarding this class was the presence of one of my own children, Beth. I also had the honor of teaching her three older sisters and her older brother in Bible class. Thus I experienced the class as a parent teaching his own child, as well as a teacher and a headmaster. I think the class enjoyed the fact that one of my children had to do all of the work that they did. We had a good relationship.

I wasn't just teaching the class for the term. My objective was to affect them for the duration of their lives. The Spirit has to do that, I realize, but I approach each class with that desire, that God would be the teacher. I have cared deeply about the spiritual welfare of the whole class, not just of Beth.

"Lord, work in the hearts of these juniors as we now part. Make them perfect and complete in all the will of God, for Jesus' sake. Amen."

Fringe Benefit Improvements

The entire faculty, elementary and secondary, met after school today to hear a report from the faculty welfare committee of the board regarding improvements being made in the fringe benefit program. The report was well received and it should be for there are marked improvements in several areas.

I think our teachers sense that the board cares about them and their welfare. The changes announced today were several months in the making. Yet through meticulous work, these improvements are being accomplished without costing the school more money, or the teachers more money.

As a member of the welfare committee, I've been amazed at the differences in what various companies offer in the areas of retirement programs, medical insurance, long term disability insurance, and group life insurance. I was happily surprised that we got better coverages for less money, for that seems impossible.

I do have one regret. If these changes had been made a year earlier they would have been a great help to the children of one of our number who, with his wife, was killed last year.

It is also true that it has taken the school years to get to the program of benefits announced today. Newer teachers can't appreciate that, but the veterans can.

"Thank you, Lord, for your care, and the care of the board."

A Godly Board President

This afternoon the phone rang and it was the board president. It's funny, but I really expected the call. The board had met yesterday to discuss a serious issue. It was a rather difficult meeting for the school has no clear policy for handling this issue, for it has rarely come up in the life of the school.

When the issue was brought up and explained, there was considerable discussion. There was good, healthy, vigorous debate, all done in the right spirit. It became apparent that there were irreconcilable differences of opinion.

After all opinions had been expressed, the issue had to be voted upon. Matters were duly moved and seconded, and the vote was taken. This was followed by prayer, after which everyone went home.

Although everything was done decently and in order, I could sense that there was a restive spirit in the board over the decision. I felt it in my own heart. This is why I expected the call today from the president. He asked me to hold up on carrying out the decisions made by the board yesterday until the board can have a special meeting next week to spend more time on the issue and come to a decision with peace.

"Thank you, Father, for a spiritual board president and for spiritual board members who realize that a restive spirit indicates that the mind of God in this issue has not been finally determined. I gladly submit myself to these people."

Faculty Family Suffering

Kenny, the youngest son of our athletic director, entered Children's Hospital today because he has been having double vision. At 10:20 p.m. his father called me to say that there will be a brain scan tomorrow afternoon at 2:30 p.m. Kenny has water on the brain and they are uncertain of the cause. It could be an infection or it could be a tumor.

After assuring George of our deep interest and prayers (we have served the Lord together at the school for 16 years now), I asked if he would mind if I came in to the hospital tomorrow afternoon just to be with Ruth and him. He said they would like it.

Peg is going too. We both know what it feels like as parents to have a son who is very sick at Children's Hospital. It is a first class hospital and the doctors are exceptional. They are also compassionate. Yet when your son suffers, you suffer too, deeply, more deeply than people who have not gone through the uncertainty of serious illness can comprehend.

I don't have any Bible text or any message for George tomorrow, and I'm sure that Peg does not for Ruth. It's just that we love them and we love Kenny and their other children. We only want to be with them in these hours of suffering. Our presence will be a way of expressing our love. Our hearts were strengthened when friends were with us at Children's.

"Lord, you are the Great Physician. Heal Kenny, please."

Thoughts During a Sick Day

The heavy cold I've been fighting for a week worsened last night. Today I stayed home from school to try to recover. As a result of prayer, medicine, and a lot of sleep today, the cold is greatly improved. It was a wise decision to stay home. (My recent schedule has been too heavy.)

Although I was not even on campus today, the school is very much on my mind. Through conversations and several phone calls, I learned of several problems, some new and some continuations. (It's funny, but I rarely get a call about something that was really good.)

I felt so poorly that creative thoughts about the school did not come to me. It comforts me to realize that the school is really the Lord's. He cares about it and he watches over it when I am not there and when I am there. I am called the headmaster, but he is THE HEADMASTER.

Someone has said that an institution is the lengthened shadow of one man. I am very eager that the shadow cast by our school be that of Jesus Christ, not that of me. Certainly I take my leadership role seriously and I want to perform it well. But I will be deeply disappointed if people think of me rather than of Christ when they think of D.C.

This is quite personal, but I never refer to D.C. as "my" school. It is his. It bears his name, not mine.

A Stressful Meeting

In a few minutes a special meeting will begin. I expect it will be very stressful. It's been on my mind with increasing concern for several days now. I know God knows the end from the beginning, but I'm still apprehensive about the meeting.

Yet I know that God is with me and that he will strengthen me. His strength is made perfect in my weakness. He is stronger than I realize — thus making me stronger than I am at this moment.

The everlasting arms are also under me. They are strong, and they are also soft and tender. (That's a remarkable thing about God.)

Several Scriptures have come to my mind. I recognize the gracious working of the Spirit in that regard. How precious is the Word in this time of severe testing.

I can't predict the outcome. I can predict, however, that God's ways are above my ways. I also know that Jesus Christ is the same yesterday, today, and forever.

"Lord, it's time for both of us to go to that meeting now."

Satanic Pressures

For the past few days I have felt strong pressures, but have not mentioned this to any of my colleagues. This morning one of them told me that he was feeling under unusual pressures. This makes me think that it is possible that we are getting more than the usual attack from Satan.

There is a difference between not feeling too good in your body and being under Satanic opposition. When there are pressures upon the soul and upon the spirit which aim to discourage or to corrupt, they obviously are not from God.

I do not want to be hyper-mystical about this, but I do want to be realistic. Satan does oppose the school. He opposes the students, the teachers, the parents, the board, and me. It would be naive not to acknowledge this, not to be alerted for this. Unusual things have happened these days. I am not wrestling against flesh and blood, but against principalities, against powers, against the rulers of the darkness of this world, against spiritual wickedness in high places.

My review of Ephesians 6 was refreshing. I am to be strong in the Lord, and in the power of his might, putting on the whole armour of God to be able to stand against the wiles of the devil. The Lord also reminded me to resist the devil and he will flee from me (James). He does not flee quickly or easily, however.

Major Discipline

Today I had to deal with a major discipline matter. The conference with parents and the student was not easy. (Actually, I can not remember a single conference dealing with serious discipline that was easy.) We talked about serious issues. There were no harsh words, probably because the Word of God was read and we prayed around before starting our discussion.

Although there were no harsh words, there was disagreement. Although there was disagreement, there was a consensus that a problem existed. We tried to focus on that problem instead of dwelling upon who said what, or who did what. We concluded with prayer.

This whole matter is grievous — to the student, the parents, the faculty, and to me. At the present it is in the most difficult stage. It will take time to tell whether the student and his parents will be exercised and change. There are obvious lessons for the faculty and for me in the matter because we could have handled some things better than we did.

The Lord brought a portion of Hebrews 12 to my mind as I reflected on this matter. That Word says that no chastening for the present is joyous, but grievous. Nevertheless, afterwards it yields the peaceable fruit of righteousness to them who are exercised thereby. I've learned that the immediate exercise is not always durable. That is why time is needed for the true colors to come to the top.

A Difficult Hospital Visit

Bud and I went to Delaware County Hospital today to visit one of our graduates. He has been out of college for two years, and teaches in another Christian School. He was married about eight months ago. Children love him. God has gifted him to teach. Everyone holds him in high esteem.

He has cancer. Evidently the symptoms came up rather suddenly — shortly before he was to be interviewed for an opening at our school for next year. From his standpoint, the timing could not be worse. For years he has wanted to come to our faculty, we have an opening, but now he is sick. (It is a rare kind of cancer, for which the cure rate is extremely low. He knows he has cancer.)

After we talked together for some time, Scott said that he wanted to ask me something. I thought that perhaps he would ask about job opportunities for future years. I was very wrong. He asked if the chairman of the education committee would bring several members to the hospital and interview him right there in his bed. (He is scheduled for what he called major major surgery in six days.) That is the dedication and the loyalty that I look for in faculty members.

I was hurting in my heart as I explained to him as tenderly as I could that he can not be considered as a candidate for next year because his health is so indefinite. Although disappointed, he understood and wants to be considered for the future. My God grant his desire.

"God, we need men like Scotty. Great Physician, touch him."

A Family Birthday

My son is 20 years old today. As I have thought of this, I remember going into the faculty meeting the day that he was born to say that the Lowries now had a quartet — a mixed quartet. (He has three older sisters and one younger sister.) Now he is half way through college.

God has been gracious in Roy's life. He has sustained him during serious illness and gives him grace daily to live above the after effects of that illness. The strength is of God.

Like his three older sisters, he is planning on teaching in a Christian school. That possibility blesses me, for I think that would be a good way for him to serve God. I'm also blessed that growing up in a headmaster's home did not turn him off toward the Christian service of his mother and father. (I enjoy the thought that someday there may be two Roy Lowries serving God in Christian schools.)

He has learned a lot already about trusting God on his own. He does not hitch-hike on my faith, but has his own. The suffering which he has experienced has worked this in his heart. He is a stronger Christian and a more mature man for his suffering, although Peg and I would not have chosen that route for him.

Again today I am reminded that God also has a Son. He knows how a father feels when his son suffers. In fact, God knows more than I, for his Son died — while mine lives.

"Father, thank you for Roy and equally for each of his sisters."

Policy on Parent-Teacher Conferences

This morning I told the faculty that from now on when a teacher has a conference with a parent about a student's discipline, the student must also be there. This comes out of a difficult disciplinary matter with which the teachers and I have been dealing. Apparently, we have made the serious mistake of talking with the student and of talking with the parent without having both of them together enough. This has allowed the playing of teachers against the parents by the student. It has put the faculty and me in a weak position. We are looking bad.

I also see clearly today that when a disciplinary problem reaches a certain level of seriousness, I must get more personally involved with the parent and the student instead of allowing the teacher and the principal to handle it. It is evident that in this matter today, I have not handled it well. In seeking to build up the authority of the teacher and of the principal, I have kept fully informed and have advised them. I've let this advisory approach be in effect for too long a time. I was not sensitive enough.

Being an administrator is a lot like being a parent. Sometimes I do well, other times I do not do well. But I have to press on and keep trying. I can't quit, because God has led me to serve him in Christian school administration. My shortcomings are always before me, for I know them better than the faculty, or the board. I must learn from them, and trust God for help, rather than allowing them to overwhelm my soul.

"Father, I'm hurt today. Help me. Amen."

Three Day Suspension

A different thing happened today — a school mother hugged me briefly in my office (I have two open doors, half glass with no curtains, in my office so anyone can look in from two directions and see me at any time) as she thanked me for the way I had spoken to her son while I was disciplining the child. The three of us had spent about an hour together. I suspended the student for three days, sent the student home with her immediately and told her that my recommendation to the board would be to place her child on probation for the rest of the year. That is strong.

During our discussion, I excused the student and spoke directly to the mother about their home and about their church. I said that her child needed the strength of a godly home and involvement in a sound church with a good youth group. The child needs to be bolstered in every way. She was open and responsive to what I said. (I wished that the father had been there too.)

As she was leaving she said that I had talked to her child just like a father, and she appreciated that. She said further that she prays for me and for my family every day. I thanked her for that. (I never take it as a light thing when anyone says that he or she prays for me and my family. The prayers of a righteous person have a powerful effect.) The thought has come to me that her prayers for me influenced her willingness to accept my counsel and the discipline.

(I have great hopes in this problem, for I saw godly repentance on the part of the student.)

A Prince with the KING

Al Wilson called at 1:30 p.m. to tell me that Pastor George Slavin went home to be with the Lord last night. I knew that he was very sick and had been praying for him. Now he is with Christ, which is far better for him.

Our Christian school movement has lost a great friend. Pastor Slavin was a frequent speaker at conferences and at individual schools. I always enjoyed his sense of humor. I remember hearing him speak at a convention one time when he ended his talk with a great joke. It was so good the people clapped. We clapped so much that he came back up to the microphone and told another joke. I got the distinct impression that he really was enjoying himself. He wasn't stuffy at all.

There was a very serious side too. His humor served to make me more open to his messages. I still remember some of the things he said the very first time he spoke at our school years ago. He had a keen way of expressing biblical truth.

In his call today, Al mentioned a personal anecdote about pastor's homegoing that impressed my soul, deeply. Toward the end, Pastor Slavin could not speak, but he wrote something to the family members who were with him. It was hard to read, but one was able to read his last words, "Resting in his everlasting arms." He was a man who lived what he preached.

"Thank you, Lord, for George Slavin."

A Restful Vacation

Things went quite well today. It helped that I am quite rested as a result of a school vacation. This time we went away for almost a week. It was great being with some of our family. It was also good not to have any night meetings or any telephone calls. The change of pace was relaxing to my mind and to my body.

Thinking back over the years, I think that I have been mistaken in not getting away more often during the times when school has been closed during the year. It sticks in my mind that the Lord Jesus even told his disciples to come aside and rest for a while. I'm not talking about "Must I be carried to the skies on flowery beds of ease...?," but just periods of rest.

One major reason, I have said, was that we did not have the money to go away. I think that I should have trusted God for that as Peg and I have for all of the other things for the family. I've noticed that when my children reminisce, they frequently talk about vacation times which were special family times.

My work is happy, but it is not easy. Only another Christian school administrator can really comprehend that. Of course, God understands that too. I like the fact that the Holy Spirit is also called the Counselor. (That's great. I'm counseled by God.)

Differences of Viewpoint

I guess that it was about 10:45 p.m. when I left school tonight. I was at a meeting of a committee of the board. It was a good meeting with a frank and open discussion of the issues. Everyone wants the Lord's will in these matters. We are friends.

During our discussion it became apparent that my viewpoint differed from that of most if not all of the committee on several points. Talking on one of those points, one of the men made a comment that I thought was significant. He said, "I don't think running a school is any different from running a business."

That frame of mind poses a problem for me, for there are differences between running a school and running a business even though board members do not always see it that way. It seems to me that the problem is this: I am under the board, yet I have more expertise in school administration than the board members under whom I serve.

This caused a few tensions tonight. I feel somewhat of a bind, because I don't want to be telling the board members what to do, and yet I must speak up and stick to what I know is correct from a school administration standpoint. I just have to live with tensions like that.

Disagreement on Discipline

An interesting discipline matter is in the works. (I'm rather wearied of discipline problems. I mentioned to Lucy today that discipline is getting harder every year, and she readily concurred.) When one of the principals called the father to discuss the problem, the father disagreed and took immediate, strong exception to what the principal said.

Realizing this, the principal told the father that he was welcome to talk to me, the headmaster, about it, and if not satisfied then he was welcome to talk to the chairman of the education committee, and if not satisfied then he was welcome to talk to the board. The principal urged the father to follow this chain.

The father's response to this counsel was, "I'll find my own channels." He said flatly that he would not talk to me.

This will be interesting because this man knows several board members well. Obviously, he intends to go to one or more of them right now instead of working through the regular channels which were pointed out to him.

It will take some time to see what is going to happen. Will the board member steer him back into the channel? Will my first call about the matter be from the father or from a board member he knows? I can't really say that the Lord has told me this, but I believe the board member will steer him to me, and that the first caller will be the father.

Family Communications

We have had a good Family Dynamics Seminar. The speaker was godly, scriptural, experienced, and well received. Everything was straightforward and practical. My only disappointment is the one that I have each year — that is, the families who needed it most did not come.

The thing that impressed me the most was a point the speaker made about communication within the family between the husband and the wife. He said that a research study revealed that the average husband and wife spend only 23 minutes per week in top quality heart-to-heart communication. I am astounded at such a low figure, and to think that that is per week and not per day. (He also said that the study was done four or five years ago, and that in his opinion the number would have declined to less than 23 minutes per week by now.)

This is a real eye-opener to me. I have recognized serious communication problems in homes where the children are having discipline problems, or where the father and mother are not getting along well. But, this shows that even the average home has a deep problem at the top level between the mother and father. That has so many implications that I can't even figure them all out.

I do know one thing though. I love Peg and thank God for our communication. I've never clocked it, but we far exceed 23 minutes per week.

Ellen and College Tuition

This was an intense day. It included two student-parent-administrator conferences for disciplinary purposes along with all of my regular administrative work. (Had an excellent talk with one of the teachers out on the parking lot on the way home. She had great insight on school issues. She also said, "I don't see how you stand all the pressures on you. I'm praying especially for you." That lifted my spirit.)

Even though it was a hard day, throughout it I found myself thinking especially of one of my own children. Ellen is on my heart. She flew to Texas last night and all day today she was visiting a

Christian School. At this very hour she is being interviewed by the school board as a prospective teacher. (I believe it is a trubute to her mother, Peg, that Ellen wants to be an early childhood teacher like her mother.)

Ellen was also on my heart as I wrote the final check for her college tuition today. Next to the entry in the checkbook I wrote P.T.L. God has helped us meet Ellen's college costs even as he did with Janet and Winnie. All of us have worked hard and prayed hard for this.

It never happened that Peg and I knew where all of the college money was coming from at the outset of any year. Yet today the final payment is in. (I've never felt that my children would suffer as a result of me doing God's will.)

"Lord, guide in this meeting with Ellen and the board. I acknowledge thy faithfulness in providing her college costs. Please use her."

Faculty Retreat Preparations

We are getting ready for our annual faculty evaluation retreat. This afternoon the entire faculty met together to list the problems which they think we should discuss during our weekend at Harvey Cedars. (Al Oldham has welcomed us there for many years. I'm sure he's never made a nickel on us with what he charges us. He believes in Christian education.) We listed problems in three areas: (1) All-school general problems, (2) elementary school problems, and (3) secondary school problems. These lists will be duplicated and given to the teachers. They will rank them in order of seriousness, return them, and a final listing according to their rankings will be issued for study prior to the weekend.

It's interesting to me that each year we have no trouble coming up with a fairly extensive list. What I really watch for is not the length of the list, but whether or not the same problem keeps coming up among the most serious as ranked by the teachers. When that occurs, it means that the problem is not yet resolved.

There was freedom of discussion in the meeting today. A similar spirit should typify the retreat. It must be like this if we are to get to the issues in these problems. At the same time, the discussions must be directed in a discreet way so no teacher is put on the spot. I don't expect the same of myself or the principals, however, because if we were administering better than we are, some of the problems listed would not be there.

"Lord, help me to be open so the teachers will be free."

Short on Prayer

For several days I've been thinking about something. I've sensed that something was not quite right, but I could not discern it well enough to really understand the matter.

Today God helped me to define this as several things clicked with me. The matter is this: Faculty members are strongly exercised right now about a certain matter, yet during our season of prayer each morning there is very little prayer about this matter.

I'm deeply concerned, now that I perceive this, that we spend hours discussing this matter together, and only a very few minutes praying together about it. The time to pray together is there, so it is not a matter of time. This marked disparity between discussion time and prayer time does not encourage me to think that this particular problem will be resolved soon.

As I reflect on this, I recall that E. M. Bounds wrote that the absence of prayer is a sure sign of work done in the flesh. It is certain that the work of the flesh will never solve the problem. What is needed is what James wrote when he said, "The effectual, fervent prayer of a righteous man availeth much."

Our faculty knows this. Tomorrow I think I'll suggest a different structuring of our prayer time after we read the Word and comment on it. My idea will encourage more peple to pray. I think it will be effective.

Chapter Three

FISCAL RESPONSIBILITY

The school treasurer called me today. The budget for next year is in the final stages of preparation. It will be presented to the board for discussion and for approval tomorrow night. (Thank the Lord for a board which is so careful in accepting fiscal responsibility.)

He called to raise a few questions with me about a particular budget account for which I am responsible. In view of the amount spent to date this year in that account, he asked if the figure for next year might not be on the high side. Is it possible to reduce the figure for next year?

I explained that the figure for the current year-to-date was lower than budgeted because of tight control on my part. The school's cash flow has been low because gift money has not come in according to the expectation built in to this year's budget. (It's always a problem to come up with highly accurate gift money figures for the budget. I've known that for years. I accept that fact as of the Lord, for the good thing about it is this: the school must trust God for its finances every single year.)

Although the treasurer did not press me at all in his questioning, I volunteered to take a 15% cut for next year in that budget account. My reason was not that I thought the number for next year was inflated. Simply put, I expect to have cash flow problems next year too, so we will again be under tight control.

A Birthday Prayer

It's 2:00 a.m. I just got home from board meeting. There are some things I want to express before I go to bed. Today (or yesterday now) is my birthday, a time for some reflection:

"Lord, on my birthday I thank you for giving me life. Thank you for Mom and Dad, that they are believers, that they taught me the gospel, that they pray for me each day, and that they are still alive. (Great chicken dinner with them tonight. And, angel food cake, my favorite.)

Thank you for Peg. Lord, she is as right for me as Eve was for Adam. Thank you for a godly, loving, understanding wife. I know I could not do what I do without her. Bless her.

And Lord, thank you for my children. I love each one so much. Each has brought great joy and enrichment to me and to Peg. Thank you for allowing me to be the father of Janet, Winnie, Ellen, Roy, and Beth. May they be upright in spirit.

Some people used to kid me about only having one son, Lord. (Few know of Peg's miscarriage of a boy between Janet and Winnie.) But Lord, you have given me three wonderful sons-in-law. Thank you for Scott, David, and Bob. Make them men of God.

Thank you most, Lord, for Jesus, my Saviour. Thank you that he is also the Saviour of my wife, each of my children, and each of my sons-in-law. I deeply appreciate this.

Even though the board meetings are so long, thank you Lord, for allowing me to serve you as a Christian school administrator. It's worth it all."

Changes in Raising Children

A parent said something today during a conference about a disciplinary matter that caught my attention. (I was glad this man came with his wife for the conference, and told him so. I've noticed that such conferences have more influence on the student when the father is there. His taking off work may have something to do with that.)

After the student had been excused, the principal and I talked alone with the parents to see if they had anything that they wanted to tell us privately. The father began to talk about the matter. It was his opinion that at least part of the problem could be traced back to the fact that he and his wife were not Christians when their oldest child was younger. He said that their younger child is different, and attributed that to the conversion of his wife and of him in the interim.

There is wisdom in this father's observation. The world does not understand biblical child training. It is reasonable that this will become evident in the life of a child whose early training is non-Christian.

Although this is true, we still have to pick up the situation where we are right now. It will be harder for this student because he was not raised this way, but he must learn discipline now. The attitude of both parents was positive, and there is much hope in this situation. It was hard because today there was chastening, which is grievous for all of us.

A Great Grandparents' Day

This was an unusually happy and exciting day at school. It was our very first Grandparents' Day. Our elementary children invited their grandparents to come for almost the whole day.

We started off with a special assembly program involving almost all of the children from K-6. (I got a kick out of one of the band numbers, "Welcome Back." Dennis, the leader, is great. He does so much for our music program.) It seemed that the grandparents especially enjoyed a physical education demonstration by about 40 children using a parachute in different formations accompanied by some snappy music.

After assembly the grandparents went to the homerooms for the rest of the morning. Then they ate the bag lunch brought by their grandchildren. Following that we had a short meeting just for grandparents. I enjoyed speaking to them briefly from Psalm 78 where the Word speaks of one generation teaching another the things of God. They were attentive.

I was surprised to learn how many came from out of state just for this occasion. We gave an award and the winner came more than 1,000 miles. We also gave an award for those with the most grand-children in the school. About eight were tied at four apiece.

As I was dismissing them, one grandfather asked if he could say something. He came up and said how much the school meant to his family. It was spontaneous, heart-touching.

"Thank you, Lord, for godly grandparents who today apply Psalm 78."

Improvement in Discipline

The faculty meeting this afternoon was unusual, for it also involved a student and the parents. I opened with prayer asking that we would all have liberty to speak frankly in our discussion and that God would grant us wisdom from above. I take James 1:5 to be workable.

That prayer was answered and there was good interchange for about an hour, at which time we concluded with prayer by one of the group. He asked God to help us all in the sequel to the conference.

During the hour it became apparent that we as a faculty and administration should have done better in the frequency and in the accuracy of our communication with the parents. There was also a problem with some of the timing in the matter under discussion. Yet there is still the problem as defined today by the participation of most of the teachers.

At the conclusion, God brought us to the best meeting of minds possible under the circumstances. Before the parents and the stu-dent left, I told them that we have learned from the situation and would do some things differently if we could start over again.

After the family left, I asked the faculty to stay for a few minutes. I spoke to them of several obvious ways in which we must improve together in handling such situations in the future. They felt the same as I.

The faculty spoke the truth in love. I'm proud of them. They handled a difficult situation with class.

Private Criticism

I had quite a bit of trouble getting to sleep last night, and slept rather fitfully most of the night until the early morning. Last evening I had dinner with some board members who asked to meet with me. As we got into discussion during the meal, (about 3½ hours worth) the talk turned rather abruptly to what they feel are my shortcomings as a Christian school administrator. (Experiences like this help me to understand how teachers feel when I have to correct them.)

It was not an easy experience. For one thing there were several of them and only one of me. That tended to skew the discussion in their direction. Also, it was hard to speak to some things that I felt were not quite right because that made me appear defensive.

All day today I have felt perplexed. I don't have everything sorted out in my heart and mind, and that is probably impossible. (God encouraged me considerably throughout the day in many ways. It is possible to serve him even when I am upset.)

One thing is clear, I must take this patiently, for that is acceptable to God. If I am buffeted for my faults, that is the way of life.

Wherein I may be suffering wrongfully, that too must be borne patiently. (I remember that I Peter says that Christ is my example.)

"Lord, help."

Pillar-like Experiences

This morning the elementary faculty invited the high school faculty to come in at 7:30 a.m. for coffee and coffee cake prior to our 8 a.m. devotions. It was a good time of fellowship and provided time for relaxed conversation before the rush of the day.

The Scripture today was Genesis 35. (I remember the day that Joan pointed out that it takes 7½ years to read through the Bible a chapter a day in faculty devotions. She had written the date next to the chapter we were reading on the first day she was at school. That's how she knew that.) My attention was drawn to Jacob's act of building a pillar in the place where God spoke to him.

I've never built a pillar but I have had "pillar-like" times in my life. As I think back, among those pillar experiences are the Sunday morning service in Springfield when I was born again, the time at

Penn State when God led me out of forestry to serve him, the day I dedicated my life to Christ at Keswick, the chapel period at Philadelphia College of Bible when God told me he wanted me in Christian camp for the summer, the time a godly woman encouraged me to be a Christian school teacher, the evening Peg told me she loved me and I asked her to marry me, the day I was interviewed to teach at D.C., the birth day of each of the children, the day Miss Traber asked me to direct Camp Sankanac, the day I was appointed headmaster of the school, the day Bill Male asked me to lead the National Institute, and others.

"Thank you, Lord, for speaking to me. I haven't built you any pillars, but I have not forgotten these experiences."

An Occupational Hazard

After supper Peg, Beth, and I were in the living room for family devotions. After reading the Word we were discussing things prior to prayer time. (I value this time greatly, for it is the highest level of communication that we have as a family unit.)

During the discussion, Beth opened up and said some of the students at school are saying some cutting remarks to her because she is my daughter. I know why. It is because discipline has been exercised, and I represent the authority in the school. The way to retaliate is to do this to my daughter. I am hurt.

I'm really sorry about this. At the same time, it would never be right to withhold discipline for fear of the backlash to my own child. I told Beth I was sorry and we all prayed about it. We didn't dwell on it after committing it to the Lord, for that is an occupational hazard that all of our children must live with without self-pity.

Although this is not fair, over the years it has been a maturing experience for each of my children. Peg and I have talked about putting them in other schools where their father was not the headmaster, where they would not have this problem, but we never felt that we should do that. They have to learn to live with some adversity, even in a Christian school.

"Father, please let these cutting remarks to Beth come to a quick end. Teach her more deeply that you are with her to help her to cope with this difficulty."

A Professor Visits

A comment shared with the faculty today brought a very obvious response of joy. Larry is doing his student teaching with us in third grade with Sue as his supervisor. (Recently Sue praised the Lord for this, for she said it is good experience for her to be a mentor for a beginning teacher. I feel that having student teachers is part of the school's ministry to "God's School System," as these students go on to teach in Christian schools throughout the world.)

Larry is a senior in a secular college. Few, if any of his profs know the Lord. Yesterday his supervising prof came for one of his regular observation and evaluation visits. Among all of his teaching, Larry teaches Bible. That presented something new to the prof.

After the observation was completed, Larry and the prof were having a private discussion about what the prof had observed. At the conclusion, the prof said, "Larry, tell me what this is about the second coming of Christ." (Boy, I think this is so good.) Well, Larry is an outspoken, winsome, young man who understands the gospel clearly and is a soul winner. He started with the question, and went from there to the gospel. The prof did not accept Christ, but heard the gospel. (Last year a supervising prof like this one did accept Christ right at school during such a visit, praise the Lord.)

In sharing this, Larry said, "I think I got one on my prof. I know something he doesn't." Later I told Larry to check out Psalm 119:99, the student's verse.

An Attitude of Gratitude

There was an exceptional spirit in our 29th Annual Banquet tonight. It worked well to put the speaker on early after the meal while people were not at all restless. Ken Gangel was here and spoke effectively on "An Attitude of Gratitude." (Come to think of it, I've never heard Ken speak ineffectively. "God bless him. I don't see how he does so much.") I like having a Christian educator as the speaker.

The message was so appropriate for us at this time. As he was speaking, I thought of God's goodness in particular to Kenny and Scotty. After thanking Ken Gangel, I invited Kenny's father and

53

Scotty's father to come to the platform to share with the audience some of what God has done for their sons, both of whom have had major surgery recently. (Scot's dad said that on a scale of 1-10, the surgery was a 10.) Both men spoke from the heart — very moving comments appreciated by all and Christ-honoring.

John, our board president, (I thank the Lord for him and for our relationship) gave out the service awards to our faculty and staff. There were three for five years, two for ten years, and one for fifteen years. After his individualized commendation, each teacher responded with a short testimony of what it has meant to serve God at D.C. This, too, was a highlight. (Next year we'll have four at 25 years, plus more.)

I concluded the banquet with short remarks of praise to the Lord for his faithfulness, which is our confidence for the future (Jeremiah 32:17).

The Basis of Fellowship

If the walls of my office could speak what they have heard over the years it would be an interesting transcript. Today I had a conference, requested by a father and mother, which touched me deeply. I've known them both and their family for quite a few years. They are mature Christians.

After our opening remarks together, the father told me why they had come. They are not re-enrolling their child at the school for next year. Both of them explained their reasons. I made some observations, but did not try to dissuade them, for it is their decision and God is their judge. (There are some times, I've learned, when a student and the school are not a good fit.)

They said they wanted to tell me this in person rather than by letter or by phone call because they love me and respect me. I'm thankful for that, for so few people come. I told them that I am sorry they are leaving, but my fellowship with them is based on the fact that we belong to one another as fellow members of the body of Christ. Withdrawal from the school does not change that.

I do not understand the ways of God as he brings certain families into the school and as he leads certain families out of the school. Each year I trust this admissions matter to the Lord, asking him to bring in the ones of his choice and asking him to also guide in the withdrawals.

This to me is in the category of which David wrote in Psalm 131. He said that he didn't exercise himself in things too high for him. I don't have to always understand things.

Traveling Mercies and Safety

A teacher asked for prayer this morning for the family of a teenaged boy who was killed yesterday in an accident at his school. I immediately asked her how the accident happened. She said that he was in the school parking lot when a friend of his drove in. Kidding around, the boy jumped up on the hood of his friend's moving car. This frightened his friend and he slammed on his brakes. The sudden stop threw the boy off the hood and he hit the blacktop on his head, suffering a mortal concussion.

I am so grieved about this. It is senseless. I don't think it had to happen. If only the dead boy had heeded the cautioning of his parents about the danger of automobiles this would not have happened. (I know some Christians don't see it this way. The Bible speaks, though, about dying before your time.)

I am also frightened by this death. Something like that could happen at our school. Prayer for traveling mercies and for safety on campus is no small request. Thank God for guardian angels. I expect to be surprised in heaven to learn how protective they have been at D.C. We also have a heavy responsibility in safety education and in daily supervision. That can not be relaxed.

"Father, I hold up these grieving parents and loved ones. Please continue to give us traveling mercies and safety on the campus. Thank you for the angels. I haven't seen them, but I know they are with us."

Singing Praises and Freedom

There is something about singing praises to the Lord together that unites hearts in quality Christian fellowship. I experienced this on a high level again this morning at the Harvey Cedars Bible Conference. On Friday night and during the day on Saturday our faculty discussed problems and sought solutions. The sessions were good, spirited.

Today, Sunday, dawned as a bright clear day, one of those invigorating days at the Jersey shore where the conference is located. Before breakfast we climbed up to the prayer tower, a glassed, turret-like room at the top of the hotel from which you can see the bay and the sea. You feel surrounded by the water.

After the reading of Psalm 150, different teachers led out with a song and we all joined in. There were not any long periods of silence, just good spontaneous singing. I think about everybody suggested at least one song. It was interesting to follow, for people were probably suggesting some of their personal favorites. (I know I did — "What Can Wash Away My Sin?")

When we had sung for about 25 minutes, we stopped for about five minutes of prayer. It was very free, very open, very hearty. Obviously the music had opened our hearts to communicate meaningfully with our God.

The worship and sharing service after breakfast was also very free as many, almost all, spoke with great liberty in the Spirit because we love one another.

Special Visit from Kindergarteners

I had just finished eating lunch at my desk when one of the kindergarten classes came to visit me. They came with Peg, their teacher, to give me a large bouquet of violets which they had picked. They sang two songs about violets and about God giving us spring.

They were enjoying themselves, and so was I. They are getting to know me better as the year progresses. Next week I'm speaking at their chapel and we'll build our relationship even closer. I love them, and like to talk to them about the Lord.

As they were with me, I had several big impressions in my heart. First, I felt again the significance of a child having his first educational experiences in a school which is Christ-centered. A beginning like that under a godly teacher means so much to a child, for he is so impressionable, so plastic.

My second impression was a racial thought. Among these children in my office were children from several different minority backgrounds. To me it is a beautiful thing to see elementary school children and secondary school teen agers of different races being educated together. For me this is a spiritual matter not at all related to the IRS regulations about tax deductions for Christian schools.

I believe that our school operates under the Great Commission. It was Jesus who told us to go into all the world and teach all nations. I don't believe that we are to do that on a segregated basis. (I know Christian educators who disagree with me. I think they have a problem.)

Parental Marital Influences

One of the elementary teachers learned some sad news today. She has observed that one of her children has been acting out of character recently, but did not know the cause. Now it has come out that the child's father and mother are having serious marital problems and are headed for divorce unless there is something that can be done about it.

(I've been quite affected by this, for I have known both parents even before this child was born. They are both Christians, to the best of my knowledge. Their marriage seemed so good that I would not have guessed what is happening.)

In talking to the elementary principal about this, she told me of several similar situations that are in progress. One child was in court recently to testify, another cried because her father has left home and has another woman. (How can that be explained to a broken-hearted child?)

My heart is moved for these children. They need an extra measure of love from us teachers, and from us administrators, because they are not getting it at home. They will never achieve up to their God-given capacities without the security of love. I know that we can not compensate for all of these home problems. But we must do something, more than we are now, for an increasing number of children and teenagers are being moved into this category by the decisions of their parents.

Personal Devotional Time

I enjoyed personal conferences with several high school students today. None was interrupted by some pressing need. There was ample time to talk to each other. There was freedom of expression in each case. (I believe they perceive that I care for them and for their welfare.)

Toward the end of each conference I raised a question about a daily, personal devotional time with the Lord. It turned out that not one met with the Lord in this manner with any consistency, if at all.

I explained some workable ideas for getting started on this and encouraged and exhorted each to do this. None resisted the idea and time will tell whether or not they will begin. (Only one said that his mother and father each has a personal time with the Lord day by day. He has a model. It will be harder for the others.)

As I've pondered this matter, I'm perplexed that so few Christian parents have a regular family devotional time, that so few parents have a personal time, and that so few fathers and mothers read the Word and pray together. It follows that these parents do not lead their own children in developing an independent time with God. This has wide implications for teaching Bible in school.

(I believe that it is possible, though, for children to rise above the practices and spiritual level of their parents because of the grace of God and because of the work of his Spirit.)

Choosing Student Leaders

The high school students are in the process of choosing student leaders for next year. They are now selecting class officers and representatives to the senate and the junior council. Campaigns are in progress.

I've been asking God to guide the students in their nominations and in their voting. Student leadership is important in the life of the school because of the intensity of peer pressure. We need leaders each year who love the Lord and are willing to stand for the right, leading their classmates in that direction. (This year the faculty and principal turned down one nomination because they did not think it would be good for that person to be an elected leader. Of course, that person is a leader anyway.)

The president of the student body has already been determined. Over the years I have seen him mature very well. He is physically impressive — a good wrestler, a heavyweight. Much more impressive is his Christian spirit. (It has been said that when God wants to measure a man, he puts the tape around his heart.) The two of us enjoy a good relationship. When I congratulated him, I told him that I was looking forward to his leadership and to working with him. (One other thing, he is black — and I like that. And, I think he likes me white.)

"God, bless Rodney and me as we have leadership roles next year."

Concerned Elementary Girls

Two elementary school girls stopped to see me before school started this morning. I was glad to see them and we chatted a bit before they told me what was really on their minds. It was plain that they were concerned about something and that is why they had come to me.

Actually, they were concerned about several things related to their school bus situation. (Sometimes I think it is a mixed blessing that the public schools must transport children to private schools too. It has raised a whole new set of problems. The other side is that some of our students could not attend the school without this busing help.)

We talked and I explained some of the things about which they had questions. The biggest thing was the fact that the driver had told them that Jesus did not die on the cross for their sins. They said he has a "different" Bible, and that it did not say that Jesus died for our sins.

I sensed the Lord's presence strongly as the three of us talked about that. The mood was serious, almost solemn. I spoke the gospel to them as clearly as I could and they concurred that this is what they believed. Then I said that all of their lives there would be people who would tell them that Jesus did not die for them, but those people do not tell the truth. They listened intently. Then the three of us prayed. It was a holy moment together.

(It occurs to me that people who say our children are too sheltered do not know what they are talking about.)

Satan Opposes Families

A school mother made an appointment several days ago to confer with me this afternoon. She waited patiently as I concluded an unexpected matter that had come up prior to our scheduled time. I apologized for the delay, and she was gracious.

As we talked, I realized that there were grave problems in the home. (That appears to be a trend in recent years in the school. Clearly, Satan is active in opposing the Christian family unit.) From prayer times I knew that the teachers had been holding this family before the Lord but had no way of knowing that the problems were so deep.

She raised numerous questions regarding the progress of her child. Some I answered, others I could not. As we talked it became apparent to me that the only way to get the total picture was to line up a conference to include the teacher, the elementary principal, and myself. She was open to the idea, feeling that it would be beneficial.

At the conclusion of the conference I led in prayer asking God for his good hand upon us. The new conference will be held in a few days.

(I was just interrupted by a school-related phone call, even though it is rather late at night. The caller has a deep need and wanted me to share in it. I've done what I could and am praying earnestly too.)

"Lord, it's time for me to go to sleep. I'm grateful that you don't sleep, but are at work all night too."

Bus Problems

An unexpected visitor stopped to see me this morning. I had never seen him before. He informed me that he was the driver of one of the public school buses which serves our school and two other independent schools. I sensed immediately that there was some trouble, for drivers never stop by for a social visit at the office.

He told me of some problems he was having with one of our

junior high students. I asked my secretary to call the student out of class to meet with us because it seemed serious enough to warrant his presence. Besides, I wanted the student to know the driver had come in, wanted him to hear the driver's complaints, and wanted him to know that the poor behaviour had to stop at once.

The student was quite surprised at the conference. As the driver rehearsed the situation, the student agreed that the behaviour had not been good. But then an unexpected thing occurred. The driver accused the student of a specific act of vandalism and immediately the student's contrite demeanor changed and there was a strong denial of guilt for that vandalism.

Now it was awkward. The driver said that he had not actually seen the student commit the vandalism. He named a third party who had seen it, however. I called the third party, and he said that the driver had misunderstood him — he had not seen the student do an act of vandalism. Thus there are no witnesses and the student denies it. I can not discipline him on that, for he is innocent until proven guilty. (God does not show me in situations like this whether or not the student is guilty.)

Prayer in the School

In reading the evening newspaper last night I was impressed by an editorial entitled, "No Time For Prayer." It dealt with the elimination of prayer from tax-supported schools and tied that to the lowering of moral standards among students today. The article was well-written by a man who serves on the school board of a tax-supported school.

The article started me thinking about the place of prayer in Christian school. My school day begins with prayer in my office and in faculty devotions. Students and teachers pray in the morning devotions. I pray as I start to teach my Bible class. Conferences frequently include prayer. The choir, the ball teams, the drama groups all pray. I've never attended a board meeting that did not include prayer.

Prayer has a demonstrable effect in the educational life of a child or of a teenager. Parents tell me every year how their children have changed for the better since being in the school. I attribute that to the working of the Holy Spirit, the grace of God, and the fact that the prayers of a righteous person have a powerful effect. (I love Ps. 116:1.)

At the end of lunch, I took about ten minutes and wrote a short letter to the editor in response to the article. I've never written such a letter before, but I did it for two reasons. First, I agree with the writer about the decline in morals paralleling the restrictions on prayer in schools. Second, I want people to know that our school believes in prayer and practices it heartily, not perfunctorily.

The Lord Himself is Coming

I saw Earl Harris to talk to this morning. It has been several years since I last saw him. (In fact, about a week ago I asked someone about him, thinking that perhaps he had died and I did not know it.) He looks good. He must be in his 80s by now.

We had only talked a few minutes when with deep feeling he looked right at me and said, "You know, Roy, the Lord is coming for us. The Lord himself, *himself*, is coming." He went on to say from memory excerpts from I Thessalonians 4 and I Corinthians 15. It was a good conversation. My spirit was lifted, built up within me.

Now the great thing about Brother Harris (Funny, but I always think of him as "Brother Harris," never as "Mr. Harris") is this: Every time I see him he reminds me that the Lord is coming again. He has been sharing this with me for many years now, no matter where we meet.

In fact, when I see him I look forward to having him exhort me about Christ's return. It is always so fresh, so vital to him that it never seems repetitious or monotonous. He blesses my soul, and I thank God for him and for others in my life who encourage me in the Lord.

(Each succeeding day my salvation is nearer than when I believed. I need to meditate on that.)

"Father, thank you for the example of Brother Harris to me. He is a man who loves your appearing. Make me like that, please."

Open House is Spiritual

Tonight was our annual Open House from 7:00 - 9:00 p.m. We registered a large number of visitors, more than last year. The student guides were kept busy. (One of the board members followed some guides to hear what they were saying to the guests. He was favorably impressed.)

I got to meet most if not all of the adult visitors by standing at a strategic spot where they entered. It was good to meet people and to answer some of their questions. There was a good spirit and the interest in the school seemed genuine. (Sometimes I have felt that some visitors really weren't interested in the school, but just came to pacify someone who had invited them.)

To me this was not just a social evening, it was a spiritual evening. All of us have been praying for God's hand to be on the enrollment for next year. Tonight was a partial answer to those prayers. Although we have an enrollment goal for next year, and our budget has been formulated on that number, we are asking God to bring the families of his choice to the school. (There is no intention of lowering the admissions standards to reach the goal.)

Trusting God in admissions is not easy. Yesterday my secretary gave me the list of families not returning next year. I never like to get that list, for it saddens me to see families leave. So, people are coming and people are going. I have to trust that to God. (I also have to be exercised and learn from it if people are leaving because they are dissatisfied with the school. There are usually a few in that category. I'm sorry about that.)

Second-Generation Students

This was a morning when the entire faculty met together for fellowship in the Word and for prayer. (On Monday, Wednesday and Friday we have separate elementary and secondary devotions. On Tuesday and Thursday we are all together.) After we read the chapter for the day and went around the circle making comments as the Lord lead, Priscilla, the teacher who led today, asked for items for praise and prayer.

I passed around the individual student prayer cards. Today we prayed for alumni. I told the faculty that it is hard to keep the information on the cards up-to-date, but encouraged them to pray for the person on their card realizing that God knows his circumstances. (I think we are always on solid biblical ground to pray that a graduate will stand perfect and complete in all of the will of God.)

Before we began to pray, Lucy made a comment about the graduate whose card she had just received that made my heart jump. She said, "I got Dan Hussar, and I just heard that he is moving to Newton Square so his children can attend D.C." (Dan, Dr. Dan for many years now, was valedictorian of our first graduating class 22 years ago.)

This year we have 28 second generation students. There is something special about our graduates sending their children to us. It blesses me to see how patiently, how graciously, how tenderly, how faithfully the Lord works in a school over the years. It is a wondrous thing to teach a new generation.

"Thank you, Lord, for letting me live long enough to teach a new generation at D.C."

The Problem of Drinking

Administering the high school becomes more complex as contemporary society is becoming more worldly. It seems to me that the attitudes of society are affecting the church, and that the attitudes of the church are affecting the school. This may be hard to discern on a year-to-year basis, but it is clear if I look at a decade-to-decade basis. (The world is diligent in seeking to press us believers into its own mold.) I can see it in the elementary school too.

These thoughts are on my heart because today I was told that some of our students were drinking after the Junior-Senior Banquet last Friday night. The banquet was well chaperoned, and it didn't happen there, but from all reports it did happen outside of the school's supervision and jurisdiction. (I take no comfort in the way it happened. They are ours.)

I'm extremely disappointed by this. Although it is hard to handle, I've started to pin down the facts and intend to talk to parents about what happened.

I've been made to understand, however, that my own convictions of practicing total abstinence are not widely held today. This creates a problem for me. I've taught this to my own children and they live by it even though four of them are no longer minors. But, although I teach my conviction about drinking, most of our students will follow the example of their parents. If their parents drink, they probably will not be convinced by my arguments.

(Praise the Lord for delivering one of our couples from injury in a serious accident after the banquet. A drunken driver hit them.)

Primary Chapel

I had two special experiences today. During the first period I spoke to the children in K-3 at their weekly chapel. (There were about 200 there. They sat on the floor and were well behaved.) They were very responsive. Talking to them about the Lord when they were so open was a tender thing to me, for I love them.

They were spontaneous. When I finished, about three raised their hands right away and asked me questions. The questions were right on the topic and were thoughtful.

A few minutes ago I got home from an evening meeting with the parents of the juniors. From 7:00 - 8:00 p.m. they talked with the high school department heads, administrators, and the guidance counselor about course selections for next year. That went well for interest was high.

We went to another room and I spoke to them about the procedures for college entrance for next year. (I told them that Peg and I are together with them in this for Beth is a junior and we are starting to talk and to pray about the choice of a college for her.)

After talking about the mechanics, I encouraged the parents to trust God and to pray regarding this.

It would be a great loss for a student to graduate and not understand what God wanted him to do next. I'm afraid, though, that there are times when that happens.

"Father, thank you for my time with the children this morning and for my time with junior parents this evening."

Prospective Teacher Interviews

I spent this evening with the education committee interviewing prospective teachers for next year. The interviews moved along well. Each was opened with prayer that God would give everyone liberty to speak with candor and that God would guide the committee in its decisions. That prayer was answered.

I have no idea how many of these interviews I've been in on, but there have been many. Each one is a fresh experience for me because the Lord's presence is apparent as we seek to know and to understand his will as we talk to each individual. It refreshes my spirit to see teachers who want to serve the Lord in Christian education. (God certainly has some choice young men and women who are coming into his School System. They speak well for the future, for they love the Lord and are bright and articulate.)

It was obvious that one person interviewed tonight clicked with the committee. I knew before we even discussed him that there would be a unanimous motion to recommend him to the board. I was right. It was great.

Usually a teacher who is offered a contract accepts, but not always. Tonight I pray that if this is of God, this teacher will accept and come to serve God at D.C. with all of the rest of us. (I will feel blessed as the headmaster to have him on our faculty.)

"Lord, thank you that you are a God who leads."

A Good Exchange Program

A nice thing happened today that I'd like to see fostered in the future. Our high school choir went to one of our fellow Christian schools and presented a chapel program. Along with the music were some personal testimonies and a short message by one of our senior boys. (Our choir director said that the testimonies gave him more insight into his own choir members, a good fringe benefit.)

What made this doubly nice is the fact that last week this school came and put on a chapel program for us. It was done well and was well received by our high school students. This simple exchange of programs has strengthened the relationship between our schools, and that on a spiritual level. Oh, we have not been in an adversary position with them. It's just that most of our contacts are in athletics where we are always competing against each other.

I don't want our students to always view other Christian schools as competitors. (I believe in good competition, and we play to win, but there is more to life than that.) Somehow we have to think of ways to deepen the spiritual relationships between the Christian schools in our area.

(Earlier in the year some friends invited Peg and me to go to a ball game between two Christian colleges. I was startled at the deep animosity between the two schools. It was unchristian.)

Dialogue with College Administrators

Several Christian college administrators were on campus this morning for their first time. I recounted the faithfulness of God to the school as we took a quick tour. It seemed to me that they were genuinely surprised at the quality of the school and of the facilities. (People often have a stereotyped idea about a Christian school and are surprised when their preconceptions are shattered by a visit to the school.)

We all went to lunch at a nearby restaurant. Steve had reserved a small room for us so that we could talk freely. At first they asked some general questions about the school. Then the talk broadened into a discussion on Christian education at all levels. It was stimulating conversation.

As we talked, they told me some things they were thinking, and I told them some things I've been thinking about Christian colleges. We all spoke candidly and easily and with a good spirit. They thanked me for their visit and for the lunch.

From this experience today I see more clearly the need to close the gap between Christian colleges and Christian schools by personal contact and dialogue between us. I need to trust God to create opportunities like this. For some reason, perhaps intimidation because I know many, if not most, Christian colleges do not endorse Christian schools, I have not been agressive enough in speaking up to college people. (Maybe it's because they want our graduates that some Christian colleges are becoming softer toward us.)

The Fine Arts

Tonight was the annual concert and art show, a special evening. The art displays were exceptional. The school's art program has come of age during the years that Gwen has been with us. She is a real art teacher. (She certainly has encouraged Beth. It was fun for Peg and me to see several of Beth's creations in the displays.)

There must have been at least 150 students in the music program. There were numbers by the beginning band, the elementary band, the seventh and eighth grade choir, the senior band, the freshman choir, and the senior choir. No wonder there was such a large crowd of parents and friends.

I'm impressed with the difference that Dennis has made in one short year as our music teacher. He has the experience and the presence. The students are responding to his high standards, which are producing excellence. (He knows of my endorsement. For one thing, I requested approval to double his music budget for next year.)

After the program Peg and I thanked many participants and were talking to parents and visitors. As we were, one D.C. father who is close to the Lord and spiritually sensitive, told me that he was praying especially for me because he knew that I have had difficult days because of recent problems at school. I took that as from the Lord and was lifted in my heart. (I'm sure there are many like him who also pray for me.)

(Peg and I went to the diner and had light refreshments and a good talk. We needed that time together, for we both have a lot on us right now.)

Scotty, A Miracle

Faculty devotions were special this morning, for Scotty Bateman came. He is a miracle of the Lord's healing abilities. (When I visited him in the hospital I would not have been surprised to see him next at his funeral.) After we sang our hymn together I asked him if he wanted to share anything with us. He took several minutes and told us some remarkable things about God. (I looked around our circle as he was speaking and noticed that several teachers were crying —the older ones who had Scott as a student and who had held him up in prayer.)

68

Scott taught my Bible class. I sat in the back of the room and he sat at the desk. His lesson was effective. The students listened intently as he spoke of some of his experiences. Among other things he said that he knew the Lord had been with him for the 24 years of his life and he was sure that the Lord was not going to dump him off at the hospital and then leave him because he had cancer.

He told also of calling the elders of his assembly and asking them to anoint him with oil and pray that God would heal him. We had studied that section of James 5 in Bible this term. What an illustration Scott is of God's power. (I need to have more guest teachers who have had deep experiences with God.)

"Lord, thank you for such a deep experience today. It rejoices my heart. Did you spare Scott so he can teach at D.C. some year? Show us."

Servants Among Servants

This was a family milestone day — our Ellen graduated from college. Before commencement this morning the president and his wife had the graduates and their families to their home for an outdoor breakfast and a time of fellowship. It was good to see some parents I knew and to meet some of Ellen's college friends.

The Lord opened an opportunity for me to have a few personal moments with the president. I thanked him for what his college has done for Ellen. (I also told him that Peg and I sent Ellen and Winnie to that college because of him. He is a godly man and I have confidence in his leadership.)

I was in a reflective mood during the commencement program. I recalled the Lord's goodness to Ellen over the years. (I remember well the morning she received Christ in our own living room.) At the same time, I tried to absorb as much of the day as possible for my memory bank.

The speaker was exceptional. I felt that God was speaking to me, too, as he spoke on, "He Took A Towel." He said that we believers are to be servants as Christ served his disciples. (He said that some people are to be servants among servants. That impresses me for my own job.)

Ellen's three grandparents were there along with the rest of the family. She knows she is loved. Bob, her husband, was gracious as we shared this day with them.

"Lord, thank you for all that Ellen is to Peg and me."

Chapter Four

SENIOR DIPLOMAS

This morning I had a personal praise and prayer meeting in my office. This is an annual event, one which I anticipate and enjoy. No one but the Lord and I know about this.

I'm referring to this — today I signed the diplomas of each senior. While doing this, I noted the name on the diploma and then praised and petitioned the Lord on behalf of that student as I was signing it. It was a deep experience, and I did not rush through it, but enjoyed the blessing of it.

I understood again the uniqueness of each senior. I know some of the gifts each has, but there are certainly gifts that will come to the fore in subsequent years. God will complete his work.

It was also in my mind that the parents of the seniors have made a great effort and have taken numerous steps of faith to give their children a Christian education. (A number of the seniors have gone from K-12 at D.C.) The Lord will honor these parents, I believe, for bringing their children up in the nurture and admonition of the Lord.

I'm looking forward to presenting the seniors to the board president on graduation night. (It is always fun to read their middle names, for they enjoy that.) Before then, we all have a lot of work to accomplish. (A few are close to the line right now.)

A Suffering Administrator Friend

Roy and I walked five laps around the track tonight. We had a good talk about several important matters as we went. (He asked me to write to him a little more often when he goes back to college after the summer.) The exercise was good and it took my mind off the main thing that is pressing me today.

I'm pressed in my soul on behalf of one of my fellow Christian school administrators. His board told him recently that if he did not resign they were going to fire him. This was dropped on him with no hint of warning, like a bomb. He has not fallen into sin and his wife and children are under control. (Evidently the problem began when he had to discipline the child of a board member.)

We had about two unhurried hours together and the Lord's presence was strong as we shared our hearts. I care for him and his family and am grieved by the unethical manner of the board. It is not right, but apparently there is no means of reversal. He and his family are in upheaval. (Several times he alluded to the experiences of Joseph, Jacob's son.)

I was encouraged by his composure, his maturity. As hard as it is, he is taking it as from the Lord and is asking him for a new Christian school assignment. (I told him that I'd be glad to be a reference for him.) He is not seeking retaliation, is not vindictive, is not stirring up the parents by phone or by letter. God will bless him, I believe, because he is taking it patiently.

"Tender Father, comfort my brother and his family. Show me how to help them. Amen."

Election of Board Members

The annual meeting of the school society went well tonight. There was quite a bit of business, but the meeting had good flow. Everyone was prepared for his part. I gave a short report, emphasizing the recent renewal of our high school accreditation for a ten year period by the Middle States Association of Colleges and Secondary Schools.

I was most interested in the election of new board members. Five men are going off the board out of 15. The five are experienced and conservative. I have enjoyed working under them and have learned from each.

The teachers have been praying about the election too. They recognize the importance of the board in the life of the school. Because the election was committed to God and because the candidates were carefully chosen, I accept the results as from God. (When all of the candidates are qualified, it doesn't matter who is elected. I see that the nomination process, then, is far more important than the final voting procedure. I'm thankful that I have a voice in the nomination process for I know the families — and they count toward a prospect's eligibility for the board.)

It is clear to me that with one-third of the board being new there will have to be more than the usual period of adjustment for me when they take office. That will be stimulating for me and I hope for them too.

"Lord, thank you for bringing these five new board members to power."

A Decision Favoring Family

I've made a major decision that I've been considering for several months. It has not been simple, but I have peace in my heart that the decision is of the LORD. (It fits something that I've told my own children and my Bible classes: It is not always easy to know the Lord's will, but it is always possible.) It was not a hurried decision, but was measured.

In my prayers, my reading of the Word, and my considerations I felt that the Lord was speaking to me in particular about the effect the decision would have upon my family. As I see it, they were primary in the decision.

Several years ago a fellow administrator ministered to me in the area of priorities. He felt that priorities should be: (1) God, (2) Family, (3) the School. I believe that. I don't think that it would be honoring to God if I am not the husband and father I should be. In fact, if I fail there, I believe that I am disqualified for serving as a Christian school administrator. (How can I work with children and young people and counsel their parents if I do not succeed with my own family?)

Some people may think that my decision was wrong. I'm not influenced by that. Before the Lord I have to do what I think is right. If I don't take care of my own, God says that I am worse than an infidel.

A Powerful Idea

("Lord, at this moment I hold before you the administrator who called me this afternoon and asked me to pray for him and his board meeting tonight. In his part of the country the meeting is just under way. Show yourself strong in these serious matters which will come up in a few minutes. Amen.")

One of our former teachers stopped to see me this morning after he had participated in the 4-6 grade chapel. It was good to see him. We had seven good years together and I was sorry when he left. Our fellowship picked up right where it left off since I last saw him, and was very free and deep as we talked of God's working in his life and in the life of his family.

He mentioned the student prayer cards that we use in faculty devotions and alluded to something I had written after hearing him pray one morning for one of my own children. (That is always a moving experience for me as I hear my own children held up before the Lord.)

Those prayer cards sparked an idea in him that he shared with me. Phil suggests that we put the names of former faculty members on prayer cards and pray for them periodically, as we pray periodically for our alumni. He said this would be meaningful to him and he would appreciate the prayers of our faculty in support of his ministry.

This strikes me as innovative, a powerful idea. I'm glad that he told it to me. I think we should do it. (A few former teachers are with the Lord — far better.)

Lying Complicates Problems

For several weeks I've been working off and on on a knotty administrative problem. This morning I had a parent conference regarding it and saw clearly the reason why the problem is complex. That reason is this: People are not telling me the truth. This keeps me from determining the heart of the matter.

(I remember that years ago I used to think that I could talk to a student and discern whether or not he was telling me the truth. How naive that was and how badly I overrated my ability to discern. One student in particular got me straightened out, for he lied to me while looking me straight in the eye with every appearance of innocence, and I believed him. The Lord emphasized to me that I look on the outward appearance and only he can look upon the heart.)

The disturbing thing about this current problem is that in this instance it is parents who are not telling me the truth. I've come to that conclusion deliberately after clear proof. It is not just a subjective feeling.

This raises a spiritual problem that could turn out to be more important than the issue which caused the conference. From all that I know, the parents are Christians. I'm perplexed by this matter. (The Lord helped me to speak frankly about the lying. I did not hold back from speaking directly.)

"Father, work in the hearts of the parents so they can counsel their children as they should."

Not Selected, and Hurt

It's funny, but my administrative instincts had alerted me for the phone call that came in mid-morning. The thing I did not know was who the caller would be. (My instincts were conditioned because almost every year I get one or more of these calls.)

The call was from a parent whose child was not elected to the National Honor Society. The parent wanted to know how the students were chosen and why this child was not elected by the faculty. My heart was touched, for the parent was crying because the child had been deeply hurt, having had induction as a personal goal without saying anything to the parents until after the special honor assembly.

Mostly I listened. Then I explained the procedures as carefully as I could. I also said that our faculty took this seriously and chose carefully. About then the parent said, "You know people call your National Honor Society some bad names." That piqued my curiosity and I asked what it was called. The parent paused momentarily and then said, "The Teachers' Pet Club." That was a new one on me. (It also stung a bit.)

"Father, comfort this disappointed family and those who did not call me, for I hear that there are others. Help these parents to lead their children in ways that will prevent backlash to the faculty. I know how parents hurt when their children hurt."

Job Definitions Needed

The Christian school administrator friend of mine who called to ask me to pray about his board meeting that night called me again today to tell me that his board dismissed him at that meeting. He was shocked. I'm shocked. He hasn't fallen into sin. When he asked the board why they were firing him they did not have solid reasons. He had not had any advance warning that his work was not satisfactory. (The last study I saw showed that the average tenure for a Christian school administrator in one school was four years. With things I've heard recently, I think it may be less than four years at this point in time.)

It appears to me that part of the problem is this: Few administrators have job definitions and standards of performance by which their boards can make a valid judgment of their performance. Lacking this, the board makes subjective judgments, which frequently are unfair to the administrator, and he has no appeal.

Earlier this year my job definition was reviewed again by the board and approved with several revisions. I'm somewhat uneasy about the definition and intend to sharpen it during the next four months and submit it again to the board. I also see the need for our board to review its own job definition, and the definitions of different committees. Our board is changing because of a large number of new members. They need good orientation and they need to understand my job too.

Special Kindergarten Program

Thank God for kindergarten children. They are on my heart because of their program tonight. It was delightful. Each did his part so well, so naturally. No wonder the parents, grandparents, brothers and sisters enjoyed it so much. (The parents certainly took a lot of pictures.)

To me the highlight of the program was the section of Scripture the children recited. They said this with feeling, not mechanically. Afterward a visitor commented on this saying that he could see that the teacher who was leading the children really felt the Scripture and had transmitted that to the children. I agreed with him. (I didn't tell him that the teacher is also my wife, Peg.)

A grandmother told me that her grandson had told her the resurrection story from Scripture at Easter time. She marveled at his perception and his ability.

The mind of a child is a wondrous thing. The heart of a child is a wondrous thing. What a wonderful time of life to teach them the Word in a natural way, integrated with all of their activities. How blessed these children are to be receiving an education in the Truth.

After the program Peg, Beth and I went to the diner for some refreshments and to unwind a bit. We had a good time rehearsing all of the things that happened in the program.

"Lord, Peg is very tired. Give her a good rest, please."

Bomb Threat

An anonymous caller phoned my office about 8:10 a.m. He told Isla, my secretary, that a bomb was planted in the high school building and that we would have one less room by this afternoon. He gave no other clues, but hung up. He spoke softly, guardedly.

Bud called the police and an officer was on campus within a few minutes. He advised that the students not be admitted to the high school building until all of the rooms had been searched. He suggested that each homeroom teacher check his own room for he would spot something unusual because of familiarity with the room. Rooms other than homerooms were to be searched by the maintenance crew.

The officer did not seem too concerned. (The other time we had a report of a bomb in the school the fire department insisted that all students be sent home at once and the campus vacated. I'll not forget that experience.) The officer said that people who really wanted to bomb the school would not give any warning, but would just do it. (That was small comfort.)

The teachers searched carefully, but found nothing. There was also earnest prayer to God for his protection in the matter. The students were not told about the threat.

It was a relief when the day ended safely and everyone was home. This sort of thing perplexes me. I don't see why the Lord permits such a foolish thing which has no rhyme or reason. Yet, in my heart I always take such a threat seriously.

A Poor Parent-Teacher-Administrator Conference

Several times this year I've observed something with some of the teachers. I saw it again today in a meeting. The problem is this: Teachers talk pretty strongly about students in the faculty meetings. This causes an administrator to bring parents in for a conference. Then in the conference the same teachers fumble the ball by not being highly prepared to talk to the parents with specific incidents which support their evaluations.

It is hardly enough now-days to say that I'm the teacher and if I say there is a problem, that's it. That doesn't satisfy parents and it really turns around and hurts the teacher because it appears to be a personality conflict between the teacher and the student. Conferences require dates and facts, facts.

Our case today was also weakened because the parents were not brought in while the iron was hot. Several weeks have gone by. True, they have been terribly busy, but still we lost the edge by not having them in promptly. Things have apparently improved a bit and it made it appear that we were talking in the past rather than in the present. That was not good.

The responsibility of this ultimately comes on me as the chief school administrator. That is the nature of school administration. I have accepted that responsibility as from the Lord. It is up to me to see that things like this are handled better next time, even though they are done by other people. If I'm disappointed, I'm sure my God must be more so.

Fellowship with Close Friends

The Lord has refreshed Peg and me during the past 24 hours by allowing us to stay overnight with a Christian couple who are close friends. Although we had not been with them for some time, we just picked up where we left off in a natural way. It is always that way when we are with them.

I think the thing Peg and I especially appreciate is the opportunity to open up and share our hearts. (It is extraordinary, but Peg and the wife are close, and I am close to the husband.) We have many friends, but do not feel as free to share things as we do with this couple. (The headmaster and his wife have to be careful — but we, too, need someone to confide in periodically.)

A lot of the closeness between our families is related to the fact that we have shared deep suffering with one another over the years. There is something about suffering that creates bonds in Christ that are far above average. To share one another's spirits when those spirits are broken knits hearts tightly.

Another reason for our closeness is that they also confide in us, making it a two way street. We are in their confidence and they are in our confidence. Peg and I know in our hearts that they love us and that they care about us and each of our children.

"Lord, thank You for these friends. We need them."

The Board Thinks Long-Range

There was a special board meeting last night to discuss long range plans for the school. The long range planning committee has been working all year and reported to the board about six weeks ago in an all day meeting. Now the board has to wrestle with some big ideas.

Before discussion, the board had its usual session of prayer. (Almost everyone always prays. There is much freedom and candor in talking with the Lord.) One man started by saying that many times the board had sat around those tables and asked for wisdom, and the Lord had given it without berating them. Another said, "Lord, as we look back the way seems clear, very plain." The way ahead is not as discernible. It never has been.

The prayers reminded me of Psalm 90, and when it was my turn I quietly prayed what Moses did, "Lord, let thy work appear unto thy servants." (I marvel at Scripture — that the prayer of Moses centuries ago could be relevant to the school today. I've noticed that same thing about other prayers in the Word.)

The meeting lasted for 2½ hours. It was stimulating, sometimes exhilarating. The ideas were large, and the spirit in which each was spoken was godly. It speaks well for the future.

"Lord, thank you for letting me serve under such a fine board, especially in light of what has happened recently in other schools."

A Crying Child

As I was getting into some desk work this morning, I thought that I heard a child crying outdoors. I went out the back door of my office onto the patio. A child was crying, but I could not see him.

I walked over to the crest of the hill and about thirty feet down the hill was a kindergarten boy, crying hard. A sixth grade girl was trying to comfort him, but he was beyond her capability. I went down, put my arm around him, and talked to him.

It turned out that he was afraid to walk down the hill to the kindergarten by himself, although that building is not too far away. The thing that had him frightened was the birds. This touched my heart, for here was a boy from the city who probably has no birds, perhaps a few pigeons, around his house. He said that he was afraid of the robins.

(I also learned that he is afraid of the squirrels on campus. He thinks that they are rats.)

I got help for him and he settled down all right. I hope that his day leveled out quickly, for he was not in a frame of mind to do very much. I certainly do not want him to be afraid to come to school or to be fearful while he is here. I've also thought that there are doubtless other children who have some other fears of which we teachers are unaware. May God give us sensitive hearts to discern the fears of our children.

Dress Rehearsal

Dress rehearsal for senior commencement was this afternoon in the gym, following the taking of the senior class picture. We began with prayer, asking God to be honored in the program and asking that the program will be a spiritual blessing to each senior.

I gave each a copy of the program and we went over it together. They were excited and it took a bit longer than I had expected. (It was not the time to be hard on them. I understand their excitement and it is warranted.)

We did the processional and recessional two times. We also went through the program again. I think that they will do well that night.

I told them that I thought it was great that about a dozen people in the class had received votes for the Timothian Award to be presented at graduation. (This honor is awarded to the student who best exemplifies I Timothy 4:12 as decided by secret ballot by the class.) There is a clear winner, however.

Nine students are giving a short personal testimony at the end of the program. They volunteered for this. After practice a tenth student came to me, almost in tears, to ask for the opportunity to give a testimony too. Since she was so earnest, I felt that I would be grieving the Holy Spirit to refuse her request. (I always enjoy graduation.)

(One boy came when practice was over. He said he thought the practice was that night. Unbelievable.)

Repeating the Grade

A father and mother came to see me today about the promotion of their child for next year. The child's teacher and the elementary school principal have both concluded that the child is not ready for the next grade. They feel it is for the child's best to be retained.

I usually have one or two conferences like this every year. They are never easy. I try to be especially sensitive in listening to the parents, and in talking with them.

I had prepared for the conference by studying the report card, learning the standardized test scores, and seeing sample work. I also went over every possible question I thought they might raise, and discussed the answer I would give with the principal. This preparation stood me in good stead, for nothing came up that caught me by surprise.

They were very gracious. I encouraged them to accept the judgment of the teacher and the principal. They said that they are considering taking the child out for a year or two, and then coming back. In this way the child would not repeat, for the secular school would put the child ahead next year. We talked about the problems in this approach.

I don't know what they will decide. It is their decision, and I did not try to make it for them. I understand that sometimes it is hard for a child to repeat. This appears to be one of those hard times, although I concur with the decision.

Good Faculty Involvement

The faculty meeting this afternoon was strong, lively, even invigorating. Everyone was involved, for we were talking about important matters. No one looked at his watch. Time went quickly.

All of the discussion was in a good spirit. There were some differences of opinion, but little was said of a personal nature that would put somebody down or on the spot. That is why the discussion moved very easily for the entire time.

Good debate is important to the faculty. It helps to reach conclusions, but it also sharpens and develops people. (The Word says something about one person sharpening another as iron sharpens iron. I have to check that out. It sounds like something that Solomon would have written.) I'm glad the teachers speak up.

The discussion was punctuated by some good humor. That kept things from becoming too heavy. The humor increased after several serious decisions had been reached. There is something wholesome about laughing together and simply enjoying one another.

Most of the faculty members have decided to have a meal together one afternoon during final exam week. School will be out at 1:00 p.m. and we will meet at the restaurant at 1:30 p.m. I'm looking forward to that. All of us will need to unwind a little by then. There is something good about sharing a meal together.

Top Visitor from the State

Something happened today that I never thought would ever happen: The man who heads up the private school division under the Pennsylvania State Department of Education came to see the school and to talk with me. It has been 21 years since anyone from the state has been on campus, and he was a staff member, not an officer.

As I showed him around campus — including the elementary school, the high school, the gyms, etc. — his comments showed that he had not expected the school to be what it is. (It seemed to alter his stereotyped idea of a Christian school. Satan lies about us so much.)

We talked in my office and at lunch about the philosophy of Christian education. He does not understand this very well and my comments were really seed thoughts. I gave him a copy of Paul Kienel's book, *The Philosophy of Christian School Education*.

It was apparent that he is aware of the rapid growth of Christian schools in the state, and in the country. We talked about reasons for this. He was not in an adversary position and showed no hostility.

He brought up the proposition that some people are expressing — that by 1990 half of the children in America will be in Christian schools. (That seems impossible to me. But, then, I never dreamed years ago that there would be as many Christian schools as there are today. God is bigger, more able, than I realize.)

God's Work and My Lifetime

The father of one of our sixth-grade teachers died suddenly this morning. We got the message during faculty devotions. Prayer time was over, but we took added time to pray for her and for the family. She will be out for the rest of the week. Our hearts are with her.

During the Bible reading in faculty devotions we read about the exodus of the Lord's people from the bondage of Egypt. The comments of the teachers were very helpful.

My attention was drawn to Joseph's bones which were mentioned in the chapter. Before he died he told the Israelites that God would certainly visit them, and when he did, Joseph said that they should be sure to take his bones out of Egypt with them and carry them to the Promised Land. They did this.

This fact is mentioned in Hebrews 11. God counted Joseph as a man of faith because he said that.

Recently I've been thinking that all of God's work at the school will not come to pass during my lifetime. That thought does not sadden me. In fact it actually blesses and refreshes me, for I know that the work is of God, not of me. Joseph did not see God's end during his lifetime, but he knew God would perform his Word. (I want to be in Joseph's band on my generation.)

Living with Uncertainty

For about two weeks now I've been living with a matter which I do not understand, for no one has explained it to me. It is of considerable importance, so it has been on my mind. I've been praying about it.

Today one of the persons involved was on campus. When the two of us were alone I asked about this matter. The person declined to explain it, saying that it had been committed to the Lord with the understanding that it would not be discussed with anyone. Since it was apparent that the person did not want to talk about it, I simply dropped the matter.

There are periods like this when things are unclear. I must live with that while maintaining balance in life. (I remember the stress placed on balance by a board member in a recent meeting. It was a good admonition for all of us.) It is not necessary to know everything all of the time to maintain balance and equilibrium. It takes trust in the living God, faith, to go on well in administration in the midst of uncertainty.

If the Lord wanted me to understand all of this matter, he could easily have opened up the conversation today. For his own reasons, this did not happen. Instead of pursuing it from some other angle, I intend to let the matter rest while continuing to trust any of the outcome to God. (The fact that there was no explanation does not change this: There will be an outcome to the matter.)

Monthly Financial Statement

This month's financial summary came to me today. The business manager and I went over parts of the print-out together. There are a few questions that have to be worked through. The report looks good. (God's good hand continues to be on the ministry of the school.)

The budget has been controlled well this year. A very few accounts have been over-drawn, but over-all we are coming in well within the budget. This is due to care in purchasing and to quite a bit of discipline in the entire business affairs of the school.

The board's fiscal responsibility is a blessing to me. They are careful and at the same time their trust is in God to provide our needs. That is a fine combination.

Another thing happened today which has underscored the value of the school's financial approach. I learned today of another Christian organization which has gotten into a serious financial position, perhaps it is even a crisis. Apparently this has happened because sound business procedures were not followed even though some sharp Christian businessmen are on the board of this organization. (The Lord's name is being hurt.) It seems that they have made a series of soft decisions without holding people accountable and the cumulative effect is going to be bad.

Today's statement is another indication that the school verse, Jeremiah 32:17, is without fault, solid.

Success Supersedes Failures

A phone call came today with an unexpected request. It is surprising. I have not even been asking the Lord to open this opportunity for ministry which was presented.

I'm certain that the person who called does not realize that his invitation carries a deep personal significance for me. There is no way that he could know this: The invitation will take me back to a place where I once failed God.

For years I have noticed that God has taken me back to places where I have failed him in prior years. It seems that he delights to give me success at those places, and I have learned to trust him rather than myself. (I never have said anything about these experiences publicly, feeling that they are intimate experiences between God and me alone.)

Already the Spirit has been ministering to me about the nature of my coming ministry at this former spot of failure. This gives me confidence that God is going to be honored in it. As I go, my own heart will be lifted up in silent praise to Him.

"Lord, I'm surprised at this. I'm nervous about it, but I've accepted. Continue to guide my spirit and my mind in preparation for this ministry. Thank you for the times you have taken me back to places where I failed You. I'm grateful. Amen."

Enrollment Left to the Student

An unexpected request for a transfer of records came to the office recently. Since its arrival I've been wondering about it, but have not felt free to question people about the reasons underlying the request. It is an awkward matter.

While talking with a teacher today, the teacher asked me if I had heard about the transfer. When I acknowledged that I had, I asked if the teacher understood the reasons. The teacher explained that it was a family matter. The father had told the child that if the child wanted to, there would be a transfer. In other words, the decision to attend the Christian school was up to the child, not the parents.

That threw a lot of light on the matter. Students who know that they can leave the school whenever they decide to never really unpack their bags mentally. They do not really settle in and learn to deal with the difficult issues of school life. When things get hard, and every student faces hard school days, they complain and blame things on their peers and on their teachers.

Parent commitment to the philosophy of Christian education is important, for it directly influences the attitudes of their children. And, children influence one another. (Peg and I feel that our own children are stronger for having to work out the hard problems they had to face from time to time in the school. It is not easy to be the headmaster's children.)

A Nostalgic Chapel

This morning I spoke in high school chapel. The seniors were not there, for they have taken their final exams and are finished with classes. This was the last chapel of the year.

It was nostalgic for me, for I have feelings about ending the year, and at the same time there is some relief when the school year is over. Never again will D.C. have the same students and teachers we've had this year, for things change. God has been good to us this year.

The students were a bit restive before chapel started. That is understandable, for they have their final exams next week and are under considerable pressure. The weather is a factor too, for it is too nice to be indoors.

My heart was moved as I stood to speak. It is such an honor to serve our students, such a privilege. I encouraged them for the last week of school, admitting that I looked forward to finishing the year as do they. Mostly though, the talk was from Psalm 15. (I love the Psalms.) The Lord had given me several thoughts from that chapter that seemed appropriate for the summer vacation period. A number of illustrations made the time go quickly. They listened well.

"Father, if my heart is moved while serving the students, yours must be too — even more so. Help each student in exams. Keep them close during the summer."

Deep Alumni Blessing

God blessed Peg and me, and the teachers, in a deep way this evening. It is hard to capture the richness in words. The occasion was an alumni dinner to which were invited the classes of 1959, 1964, 1969, and 1974. It was so good to renew fellowship with those who were able to come, and to meet their spouses.

Some went to great efforts to come. One couple came all the way from California and one from Mexico. Others were missionaries home on furlough from Taiwan and a naval aviator from Florida. As punch was served we all got to move around and do some quality visiting. The meal was tasty, the fellowship extraordinary.

The alumni president asked me to say a few words. I reminisced a bit and updated them on the progress of the school. (Some of them were amazed at the new buildings which have been completed since their days.) I then assured them that the changes at D.C. have been those of facilities, not those of purpose. Our Christian philosophy and our spiritual objectives have not changed.

Then I concluded by expressing our continued interest in them as demonstrated through the prayers of the faculty for individual alumni every Tuesday and Thursday morning. (Their names are on individual prayer cards.)

"Father, thank you for such a special evening. My soul is refreshed and I know Peg's is too. Amen."

Commencement

The school's twenty-second commencement was tonight. Every one has its own character and its own blessings. Different people are probably touched in different ways as the Spirit ministers during the program.

The people on the program met for orientation and prayer in my office before the processional. Our prayer time was very free as we asked God to get honor to himself tonight.

The salutatory address and the valedictory address were good. So was the main address. (It was not too long either.)

Five, ten, and fifteen year awards were presented to six of our faculty and staff. A book was presented to a pastor and his wife whose sixth child was in the graduating class. (They now have four grandsons in the school.)

At the end of the program, as the headmaster of the school I reaffirmed the school's intent to honor Jesus Christ. I spoke of Christ and of our commitment to the Scripture. (This was special to me, although only a few sentences.)

One special thing — it was my privilege to represent the board in honoring the president, who is retiring. I think that he was surprised to receive a fine plaque which included the names of all of the board members.

Peg and I went through the receiving line and said goodby to each of the graduates. They are our life. We love them, and will miss them.

"God, guide the graduates as long as they live. Amen."

Caution During the Last Week

The last week of school for this year began this morning. All of us are tired, and are looking forward to the end. There are extra activities going on in the elementary school — class picnics, showers for teachers getting married this summer, etc. High school final examinations begin tomorrow. (Worth 20% on the semester grade.)

Over the years the Lord has taught me not to let down my spiritual guard during the last week. He emphasized that to me again today when something very discouraging came out of the blue. (Satan is clever, a good strategist.)

In morning devotions we read about the Lord helping Joshua and the Israelites as they fought Amalek. When Moses held his hands in the air, Joshua prevailed. Two men held his hands up, with the rod, when he tired. God said to record that and rehearse it to Joshua, probably to make sure the credit for the victory was given to God rather than Joshua.

In the chapter, the Lord is called by his name, Jehovah-nissi, the Lord our banner. In this discouragement of today, my confidence is in Jehovah-nissi. The issue requires his resolution. Though I will be involved completely, I look to him, confidently.

Jesus has promised never to leave me nor forsake me, so that I may boldly say the Lord is my helper. I will not fear what man can do to me.

Year-end Conferences

A parent had made an appointment with me for today to look at the permanent record folder of a child. (I had one of the other administrators with me in case a question came up.) The parent read almost everything carefully. It took about an hour. The parent did not say what information was being sought. Upon completion of the review, the parent thanked me, said nothing of the intent of the study, and left. (I have a feeling that there has to be more to it. Time will tell.)

A second parent came in for an appointment around noon. I had talked to his child's teacher and to the elementary school principal and was highly prepared. I even had the child's permanent records in the office in case certain questions might come up. I asked the teacher what questions I should expect.

As it turned out, this father was congenial as we talked together about his son repeating kindergarten next year. (I've observed that this is often hard for parents to accept, especially fathers.) We discussed the reasons and the advantages. I'm sure these had been explained by the teacher. Perhaps it helped him to hear it from another man. We concluded on a positive note. It is not a borderline decision. The child just needs more time to mature. (Sometimes parents are in a hurry for their children to grow up. God is not in a hurry.)

An Appreciation Luncheon Surprise

After exams at 1:00 p.m. the Mothers' Service Club gave a beautiful "Appreciation Luncheon" for all of the faculty and staff. The food was good, the tables nicely decorated, and the fellowship very close. Looking around the room, it was obvious that people were enjoying it. The timing was right.

When the luncheon was concluding, I presented engraved plaques to faculty and staff who had completed 5, 10, and 15 years at D.C. There were six. Then, to my surprise, Lucy called me up front and gave me a gift from the faculty and staff in honor of my 25th year as headmaster of the school. (She admonished me that Moses lead the people for 40 years and told me that I still have a long way to go.)

The gift is a beautiful color picture of the front door of the original building. That is very significant to me. As I thanked the teachers, I asked them to further personalize it by signing their names on the back of it. (I treasure this — front and back — right now, and will in years to come.) Then Bud presented another gift, a beautiful clock. How kind of them. (We love each other.)

Tonight I went to a Phillies baseball game. It was relaxing. When I got home, Peg told me that my father had to go into the hospital suddenly while I was at the game.

"Father, watch over my father, please. Heal him I ask. Our eyes are unto you."

An Up-Dated Discipline Policy

Bud and I worked hard on what I hope will be the last revision of the up-dated discipline policy. This must be about the fourth draft this year and it has been in the works longer than that. The teachers have debated it on the elementary school level and on the secondary school level. The teachers have also had the opportunity to write parts of it in committees and individually. Now we are at the point of editing it, which cannot be done by a group. (Lucy is also involved.)

The policy looks good, but is wordy. About 20% can be cut without changing the meaning. Upon completion it will go to the education committee and then on to the board. There are bound to be some differences of opinion. Hopefully they will be minor. (I'm pushing to get this done tomorrow, for I do not want it to carry over into the summer.)

After exams today the high school faculty went to the Newtown Squire for lunch. Almost everyone went. It was fun to enjoy a hot meal together with waitress service after brown-bagging it all year. We even had a private room. The fellowship was easy, relaxed.

(Tonight I picked up my mother and we went to Lankenau Hospital to visit Dad. He is uncomfortable. They did not do much today but he is scheduled for some important tests tomorrow. Surgery seems probable. "God, help Dad in these tests. Guide the doctors. Touch him.")

Last Day of School

It is 1:40 a.m. I just got home from the board meeting. (Roy and Beth leave in 4 hours and 20 minutes for New Hampshire, where they will serve the Lord for the summer at Camp Brookwoods and Camp Deer Run.) Today, yesterday now, was the last day of school for this year. It went well even though everyone was excited.

The last of the purchase orders for next fall were on my desk this morning. I signed them and thanked the secretaries in the business office for completing a tedious job well. (They always do good work.)

Supper tonight was a great family time. We ate at the picnic table and enjoyed each other as well as a great meal.

I knew that a hard thing was coming up at the board tonight, and had some time alone with the Lord before going to the meeting. During board devotions the Spirit brought to my mind the song taken from Scripture, "The joy of the Lord shall be my strength." That really lifted my spirit and I found myself singing it in my mind several times during the meeting.

The problem part of the meeting went as well as could be expected. I hope that it is over now and does not go on into the summer.

The board passed a resolution thanking me for the completion of my 25th year as headmaster of D.C. (300 regular board meetings and an unlimited number of special board meetings and committee meetings.)

Lord...

I went out to lunch today because school is out for the summer and because visitors came to see me. We were having a relaxed meal when the waitress surprised me by telling me that I had a telephone call. As I walked to the phone I sensed that there was trouble. I never get a call at a restaurant.

My secretary was on the phone, but when I answered she gave the phone to one of the principals. He gave me this news — a teacher who just finished her first year of teaching with us committed suicide last night at the summer camp where she had gone to work. They found her body this morning.

The rest of the meal was blurred. I could hardly talk from the shock. The group went back to school and I excused myself at once and went to the office.

Soon the teacher's father was on the phone. Both of us were crying. We made fairly firm plans to have her memorial service in the school gym three days from now. I offered to line up the special music, the ushers, etc. Her pastor will speak. (A hard assignment under the circumstances.)

The whole thing is such a surprise. The teacher spoke to me warmly before leaving for the summer. She said she was looking forward to next year. (How will I explain this to my daughter, Beth, who has already gone to summer camp? Beth loves this teacher, for she was her varsity coach.) I had no idea she was depressed like this, let alone suicidal.

"Oh, God, what is this? What could I have done? Why didn't she tell me? Strengthen me for this hard summer. And prove yourself gentle to my own Beth when I call and crush her with this."

SPECIAL BIBLIOGRAPHY

This is not a typical bibliography, for the book does not lend itself to that. To compile this, I wrote to some people in Christian education who have been a godly influence on me and asked them to list the three books apart from the Word of God (obviously first) which have had the greatest impact on their lives. I thought this would be a highly significant selection of books.

It was not a simple request, as several mentioned. Joe Bayly, for example, said,

"...You have given me a difficult assignment. To list the three books, apart from the Bible, which have influenced me the most is almost impossible. The reason for this is that various books had great influence in my childhood, my youth, and the various ages since." (Joe Bayly interviewed me along with his education committee members, and hired me to serve God at D.C.)

The bibliography is presented with appreciation to the persons contributing, and with the desire that the books influencing them will have a similar effect on others.

Joseph T. Bayly, Vice President, David C. Cook Publishing Co., Elgin, Illinois

Heywood, Robert B., ed. **The Works of the Mind.** Chicago: University of Chicago Press, 1947. Phoenix ed. 1966.

Ibsen, Henrik. **Brand.** Michael Meyer tr. New York: Doubleday, n.d.

Tournier, Paul. **The Meaning of Persons.** New York: Harper and Row, 1957

James W. Braley, Director of Educational Services, Association of Christian Schools International, Whittier, California

Blamires, Harry. **The Christian Mind.** London: S.P.C.K., 1963.

Byrne, H. W. **A Christian Approach to Education.** Milford, Michigan: Mott Media, 1961, 1977.

Getz, Gene A. **Building Up One Another.** Wheaton: Victor Books, a division of Scripture Press Publications, Inc., 1976.

J. Lester Brubaker, Superintendent, Lancaster Mennonite High
School, Lancaster, Pennsylvania

> Black, Hugh. **Friendship.** New York: Fleming H. Revell
> Company, 1903.

> Paton, Alan. **Cry, the Beloved Country.** New York: Charles
> Scribner's Sons, 1948.

> van Bright, Thieleman J. **Martyrs Mirror.** Scottdale: Herald
> Press, 1950. First published in Dutch in 1660.

Ron Chadwick, Professor, Baptist Theological Seminary, Grand
Rapids, Michigan

> Clark, Gordon. **A Philosophy of Christian Education.** Grand
> Rapids: William B. Eerdmans, 1946.

> Gaebelein, Frank E. **The Pattern of God's Truth.** New York:
> Oxford University Press, 1954.

> LeBar, Lois E. **Education That Is Christian.** Westwood, New
> Jersey: Fleming H. Revell Co., 1958.

A. C. Fortosis, Professor, Christian School Administration, Grand
Rapids Baptist Seminary, Grand Rapids, Michigan

> Blamires, Harry. **The Christian Mind.** London: S.P.C.K., 1963.
> O'Hallesby. **Prayer.** London: Hodder & Stoughton, 1936.

> Schaeffer, Francis. **The God Who Is There.** Downers Grove,
> Illinois: InterVarsity Press, 1968.

> Smith, Hannah W. **Christian's Secret of A Happy Life.**
> Westwood, New Jersey: Fleming H. Revell Co., 1952.

Frank E. Gaebelein, Headmaster Emeritus, The Stony Brook
School, Stony Brook, Long Island, New York

> Bunyan, John. **The Pilgrim's Progress.** Part I, 1678; Part II,
> 1684.

> Pascal, Blaise. **Pensees.** Everyman's Library, No. 874.

> Speer, Robert E. **The Finality of Jesus Christ.** Channel Press.

Kenneth O. Gangel, President, Miami Christian College, Miami,
Florida

> Chafer, Lewis S. **He That Is Spiritual.** Wheaton, Illinois: Van
> Kampen Press, 1918.

Elliott, Jim. **The Journal of Jim Elliott.** Old Tappan: Fleming H. Revell Co., 1978.

Gaebelein, Frank E. **The Pattern of God's Truth.** Chicago: Moody Press, 1968.

Schaeffer, Francis. **How Should We Then Live?** Old Tappan: Fleming H. Revell Co., 1976.

Gene Garrick, Pastor, The Tabernacle Church, Norfolk, Virginia

Gaebelein, Frank E. **The Pattern of God's Truth.** Chicago: Moody Press, 1968.

Small, Dwight E. **Design For Christian Marriage.** Old Tappan: Fleming H. Revell Co., 1959.

Tozer, A. W. **Pursuit of God.** Harrisburg: Christian Publications, Inc., 1948.

Maynard L. Gray, Principal, Delaware County Christian School, Newtown Square, Pennsylvania

Elliott, Elizabeth. **Shadow of the Almighty.** New York: Harper, 1958.

Tozer, A. W. **Pursuit of God.** Harrisburg: Christian Publications, Inc., 1948.

Ruth C. Haycock, Professor, Christian Education, Piedmont Bible College, Winston-Salem, North Carolina

Gaebelein, Frank E. **The Pattern of God's Truth.** Chicago: Moody Press, 1968.

Havergal, Frances R. **Kept For The Master's Use.** New Canaan: Keats Publishing , Inc.

Laidlaw, Robert A. **The Reason Why.** Grand Rapids, Michigan: Zondervan, 1970.

Taylor, Howard, Dr. & Mrs. **Hudson Taylor's Spiritual Secret.** Chicago: Moody Press, 1932.

Lucille Johnston, Elementary Principal, Delaware County Christian School, Newtown Square, Pennsylvania

Alden, Raymond M. **Why The Chimes Rang.** Bobbs Merrill Company, 1906.

Evans, A. R. **Wilfred Grenfell.** Grand Rapids, Michigan: Zondervan Publishing House, 1954.

Keller, Helen. **The Story of My Life.** New York: Doubleday & Co., 1954.

Paul A. Kienel, Executive Director, Association of Christian Schools International, Whittier, California

Schindler, Jr. Claude E. **Educating for Eternity.** Wheaton, Illinois: Tyndale House.

Sheley, Donald B. **Beggar at the Banquet.** San Bruno, California: Privately Published.

Maribel Kraybill, Principal, Locust Grove Mennonite School, Smoketown, Pennsylvania

Chambers, Oswald. **My Utmost For His Highest.** Dodd-Mead & Company, 1964.

Dresher, John. **Spirit Fruit.** Scottdale, Pennsylvania: Herald Press, 1974.

Sanders, J. Oswald. **Spiritual Leadership.** Chicago: Moody Press, 1967.

Taylor, Jack R. **Prayer: Life's Limitless Reach.** Nashville: Broadman Press, 1977.

Ron Krestan, Superintendent, Kansas City Christian Schools, Merriam, Kansas

Byrne, H. W. **A Christian Approach To Education.** Milford, Michigan: Mott Media, 1977.

McConkey, Dale D. **MBO For Nonprofit Organizations.** New York: Amacom, American Management Association, 1976.

Nash, Paul. **Models of Man, Explorations in Western Educational Tradition.** New York: John Wiley and Sons, Inc., 1968.

E. William Male, Dean, Grace Theological Seminary, Winona Lake, Indiana

Machen, J. Gresham. **Christianity and Liberalism.** Grand Rapids: Wm. B. Eerdmans Publishing Co., 1946.

Spurgeon, C. H. **Lectures to my Students.** London: Marshall, Morgan & Scott, 1954.

Gaebelein, Frank E. **Christian Education in a Democracy.** New York: Oxford University Press, 1951.

Robert Miller, Superintendent, Norfolk Christian Schools, Norfolk, Virginia

Gaebelein, Frank E. **The Pattern of God's Truth.** Chicago: Moody Press, 1968.

Sanders, J. Oswald. **A Spiritual Clinic.** Chicago: Moody Press, 1958.

Sanders, J. Oswald. **Spiritual Leadership.** Chicago: Moody Press, 1967.

Charles Schauffele, Professor, Christian Education, Gordon-Conwell Theological Seminary, South Hamilton, Massachusetts

Blamires, Harry. **The Christian Mind.** London: S.P.C.K., 1963.

Bunyan, John. **Pilgrim's Progress.** New York: Penguin Books.

Murray, John. **Principles of Conduct.** Grand Rapids, Michigan: William B. Eerdmans.

Zylstra, H. **Testament of Vision.** Grand Rapids, Michigan: William B. Eerdmans.

John Schimmer, Director of South Central Region, Association of Christian Schools International, Dallas, Texas

Blamires, Harry. **The Christian Mind.** London: S.P.C.K., 1963. Now available: Servant Publications, 237 North Michigan, South Bend, Indiana 46601.

Packer, J. I. **Knowing God.** Downers Grove, Illinois: Inter-Varsity Press, 1973.

Spurgeon, Charles Haddon. **Lectures to my Students.** Grand Rapids, Michigan: Zondervan, 1954.

Robert Siemens, Headmaster, Loudonville Christian School, Loudonville, New York

Chafer, Lewis Sperry. **He That Is Spiritual.** Chicago: Moody Press, 1918.

Springer, E. Laurence. **Independent School Administration.** New York: Harper and Row, 1967.

Taylor, Howard. **Hudson Taylor's Spiritual Secret.** London: China Island Mission.